Ahmad Alkhatib

Lactate, carbohydrate and fat utilisation during exercise

Ahmad Alkhatib

Lactate, carbohydrate and fat utilisation during exercise

Interrelationship, and applications in exercise testing

LAP LAMBERT Academic Publishing

Impressum/Imprint (nur für Deutschland/ only for Germany)

Bibliografische Information der Deutschen Nationalbibliothek: Die Deutsche Nationalbibliothek verzeichnet diese Publikation in der Deutschen Nationalbibliografie; detaillierte bibliografische Daten sind im Internet über http://dnb.d-nb.de abrufbar.

Alle in diesem Buch genannten Marken und Produktnamen unterliegen warenzeichen-, marken- oder patentrechtlichem Schutz bzw. sind Warenzeichen oder eingetragene Warenzeichen der jeweiligen Inhaber. Die Wiedergabe von Marken, Produktnamen, Gebrauchsnamen, Handelsnamen, Warenbezeichnungen u.s.w. in diesem Werk berechtigt auch ohne besondere Kennzeichnung nicht zu der Annahme, dass solche Namen im Sinne der Warenzeichen- und Markenschutzgesetzgebung als frei zu betrachten wären und daher von jedermann benutzt werden dürften.

Coverbild: www.ingimage.com

Verlag: LAP LAMBERT Academic Publishing AG & Co. KG
Dudweiler Landstr. 99, 66123 Saarbrücken, Deutschland
Telefon +49 681 3720-310, Telefax +49 681 3720-3109
Email: info@lap-publishing.com

Herstellung in Deutschland:
Schaltungsdienst Lange o.H.G., Berlin
Books on Demand GmbH, Norderstedt
Reha GmbH, Saarbrücken
Amazon Distribution GmbH, Leipzig
ISBN: 978-3-8383-3891-0

Imprint (only for USA, GB)

Bibliographic information published by the Deutsche Nationalbibliothek: The Deutsche Nationalbibliothek lists this publication in the Deutsche Nationalbibliografie; detailed bibliographic data are available in the Internet at http://dnb.d-nb.de.

Any brand names and product names mentioned in this book are subject to trademark, brand or patent protection and are trademarks or registered trademarks of their respective holders. The use of brand names, product names, common names, trade names, product descriptions etc. even without a particular marking in this works is in no way to be construed to mean that such names may be regarded as unrestricted in respect of trademark and brand protection legislation and could thus be used by anyone.

Cover image: www.ingimage.com

Publisher: LAP LAMBERT Academic Publishing AG & Co. KG
Dudweiler Landstr. 99, 66123 Saarbrücken, Germany
Phone +49 681 3720-310, Fax +49 681 3720-3109
Email: info@lap-publishing.com

Printed in the U.S.A.
Printed in the U.K. by (see last page)
ISBN: 978-3-8383-3891-0

TABLE OF CONTENTS

CHAPTER ONE: Literature Review

DEFINITION OF TERMS AND ABBREVIATIONS

ATP	Adinosine tri-Phosphate
ADP	Adinosine diphosphate
AMP	Adinosine monophosphate
BLC	Blood lactate concentration
Ca^{+2}	Calcium
CPT-I	Carnitine palmitoyltrasferase-I
CO_2	Carbon Dioxide
EE	Energy expenditure
FFA	Free Fatty acid
Fatmax	Maximal fat oxidation
H^+	Hydrogen ions
HG	Handgrip protocol
kel	Constant of half maximal pyruvate combustion
LCFA	Long chain fatty acid
LDH	Lactate dehydrogenase
LT	Lactate threshold
MLSS	Maximal lactate steady state
NAD	Nicotinamide adenine dinucleotide
NG	Non-gripping protocol
O_2	Oxygen
Pi	Phosphate
PCO_2	Carbon dioxide pressure
PDH	Pyruvate dehydrogenase
PO_2	Oxygen pressure
PYR	Pyruvate oxidation rate
RER	Respiratory exchange ratio
RFAT	Relative rate of fat utilisation
rpm	Revolution per minute
RPY	Relative rate of pyruvate combustion
RQ	Respiratory quotient
TG	Triglycerides
$\dot{V}_E$	Minute ventilation

$\dot{V}O_2$ Oxygen uptake

$\dot{V}CO_2$ Carbon dioxide production

$\dot{V}O_{2peak}$ Peak oxygen uptake

$\dot{V}O_{2\,max}$ Maximal oxygen uptake

$\%\ \dot{V}O_{2peak}$ Relative exercise intensity to peak oxygen uptake

LIST OF FIGURES

LIST OF TABLES

LISTS OF EQUATIONS

DEDICATION AND ACKNOWLEDGMENT

I would like to dedicate this book to the loving memory of my father, Murshed who passed away whilst I am writing this work. With his warm support, and encouragement I was always inspired.

Thanks for my family for being always there for me throughout. Thanks to all of my friends for their great encouragement. Special thanks to Prof. Ralph Beneke for his guidance and support throughout this project. Finally, thanks for all the participants who volunteered to take part in the experiments.

CHAPTER ONE
LITERATURE REVIEW

1.1. THE EFFECTS OF EXERCISE INTENSITY ON ACUTE PHYSIOLOGICAL RESPONSES

This section describes the effects of exercise intensity on ventilatory responses of oxygen uptake ($\dot{V}O_2$), carbon dioxide production ($\dot{V}CO_2$), blood lactate, and the substrate utilisation of carbohydrate (CHO) and fat. The following literature review examines these physiological responses to exercise at both local muscle, and whole body levels. The main focus of this book is the response of the whole body level.

Exercise intensity refers to how hard the body is working during physical activity. Exercise intensity is mostly represented as the external power output measured in watts (W). This becomes meaningful when considering the corresponding $\dot{V}O_2$ response which includes the internal work or the resting metabolic rate. Exercise intensity is commonly used in relative terms to $\dot{V}O_{2peak}$ as (% $\dot{V}O_{2peak}$), or to peak power output (%). Both terms will be used within this book, with it important to state that % $\dot{V}O_{2peak}$ is higher than % peak power as it includes resting metabolic rate in its percentage.

1.1.1. Effects of exercise intensity on oxygen uptake and carbon dioxide output:

Exercise intensity determines different respiratory responses of $\dot{V}O_2$ consumption and a corresponding $\dot{V}CO_2$ production. The oxygen cost of performing work depends on the work rate. In an incremental exercise test $\dot{V}O_2$ essentially increases linearly as exercise intensity increases. Jones and Pool (2005) reported a $\dot{V}O_2$ slope of 10 ml.min.W^{-1} in a 3-min stage incremental test for trained subjects. This linear relationship of $\dot{V}O_2$ power output was not changed by altering the incremental test protocol in terms of the increment size and workload or subjects' fitness level (Beaver *et al.* 1986; Howley *et al.* 1995; Wasserman *et al.* 2005; Jones and Poole 2005).

In constant work load tests three temporal components characterise the $\dot{V}O_2$ response and are reportedly divided into moderate, heavy and severe intensity domains (Gaesser

1

and Poole 1996). Some investigators have divided the $\dot{V}O_2$ responses into four by adding the very heavy exercise intensity domain (Ozyener et al. 2001). Furthermore, the time course of the change in $\dot{V}O_2$ response within each intensity domain has also been characterised and attributed to a different stimuli. Three temporal components characterises the $\dot{V}O_2$ response: a) the early, usually rapid response; b) the slower, exponential increase; and c) the steady state (Whipp 1994). In healthy subjects, it takes approximately 30s to attain 63%, 60s to attain 86%, and 120s to attain 98% of the steady state amplitude of $\dot{V}O_2$ (Jones and Poole 2005). A steady state attainment of $\dot{V}O_2$ of > 99%, is reached by approximately 3 min at moderate exercise intensity. At higher intensities in the heavy and severe domains, $\dot{V}O_2$ continues to increase beyond the 4th min, and so, the rate at which $\dot{V}O_2$ increases is greater the higher the work rate, and an influence of a slow component is expected in the heavy, and severe intensity domains (Jones and Poole 2005). $\dot{V}O_2$ continues to increase in the severe exercise intensity until the point of fatigue, and the maximum level of $\dot{V}O_2$ (VO_{2max}) is attained at the end of exercise (Xu and Rhodes, 1999).

$\dot{V}CO_2$ during exercise comes from three sources: a) aerobic metabolism, which is linearly related to $\dot{V}O_2$; b) bicarbonate buffering of lactic acid; and c) acute hyperventilation as respiratory compensation of pulmonary capillary blood (Stringer et al. 1995). Therefore, $\dot{V}CO_2$ response is similar to that of $\dot{V}O_2$ below lactate threshold (LT) but increases disproportionately at higher intensities above LT. $\dot{V}CO_2$ was mostly described using two regression lines as in the commonly used V-slope method for the estimation of anaerobic threshold (Beaver et al. 1986), though some investigators do not support the existence of a threshold (Yeh et al. 1983). Furthermore, $\dot{V}CO_2$ was also described as an exponential function of exercise intensity (Dennis and Noakes 1998).

$\dot{V}CO_2$ is considered to reach a steady state after approximately 3 min depending on exercise intensity (Stringer et al. 1995). It has been argued that $\dot{V}CO_2$ has a slower response than that of the $\dot{V}O_2$ at moderate and heavy exercise intensity domains. This is reflected by a lower delay time and a lower time constant for $\dot{V}CO_2$ compared with that of $\dot{V}O_2$ as shown in Bell et al. (1999), and explained in details by Whipp and Ward (1993)..

2

Increased exercise intensity elicits increases in $\dot{V}O_2$ and $\dot{V}CO_2$, reflecting the following mechanisms (Wasserman *et al.* 2005):

1) Increase in $\dot{V}O_2$ needed to satisfy the increased work of respiratory muscles and the heart at high ventilatory and cardiac output responses.
2) Increased recruitment of fast-twitch muscle fibres.
3) Increased muscle recruitment in terms of muscle groups and number.
4) Acidemia facilitating O_2 unloading from haemoglobin by shifting the oxyhaemoglobin dissociation curve downward for a given PO_2.
5) Progressive vasodilatation to the local muscle units by metabolic vasodilators (e.g. high H^+ gradient, High PCO_2, low PO_2), thereby, increasing O_2 flow and consumption at O_2 deficient sites.
6) The O_2 cost of converting lactate to glycogen in the liver, as the lactate concentration rises, is also contributory.

1.1.2. Lactate response to exercise intensity:

At physiological pH, lactic acid almost completely dissociates to hydrogen and lactate ions, therefore the terms lactic acid and lactate are often used synonymously. However, when describing lactate-lactic acid transport across membranes precise terminology is required (Brooks 1985).

Blood Lactate Concentration (BLC) response is mainly dependant on exercise intensity and duration. In incremental load tests lactate response remains similar to its resting levels or increases slightly at low exercise intensities. However, BLC starts to increase abruptly at any intensity between about 40-80% $\dot{V}O_{2peak}$. BLC is dependant on work load essentially, but highly related to exercise duration, fitness level, age, and cardiovascular disease status (Wasserman *et al.* 2005). Attempts to fit lactate response to exercise intensity focused mainly on the intensity at which BLC threshold is achieved, and many mathematical models have been introduced for this purpose (Beaver *et al.* 1986; Wasserman *et al.* 1990).

The main two approaches describing BLC response to exercise were the bilinear model (Beaver *et al.* 1986) and the mono-exponential model introduced by Hughson *et al.* (1987). Wasserman *et al.* (1990) argued that the bilinear model fits the BLC data better than the exponential at intensities corresponding to BLC values below 4.5 mmol.l^{-1}. This is mainly because of better distribution of the parameters' extremes being estimated. However, others suggest that the progressive proton production from carbohydrate oxidation is progressively accelerated, and therefore, a 3-parameter mono-exponential is preferred over a bilinear model for describing BLC, $\dot{V}CO_2$, and may be $\dot{V}O_2$ (Dennis *et al.* 1992).

The level of increment size and duration have a clear effect on BLC attainment of a steady state (Stockhausen *et al.* 1997). Therefore, some investigators suggested performing constant load tests lasting longer than 20 min at several exercise intensities, to determine the time course of BLC (Beneke and vonDuvillard 1996; Beneke 2003b; Billat *et al.* 2003).

1.1.2.1. Mechanisms of lactate increase and accumulation:

The traditional role of lactate has been known as follows (Gladden 2000): a) the immediate energy donor for muscle contraction; b) a primary factor in muscle soreness; c) the central cause of O_2 debt; and d) a causative agent in muscle fatigue. However, significant changes to the understanding occurred over the past 30 years, and the most widely believed explanations become as follows:

1) Cell redox: Traditionally it was argued that muscle and blood lactate concentrations increase with exercise intensity because of inadequate O_2 supply to the exercising muscles (muscle hypoxia) since the era of Hill et al. (1924). This belief was developed later that century by Margaria *et al.* (1933), whom suggested that lactate increase during exercise was related to the O_2 debt. This theory is currently considered and strongly supported by several experiments (Wasserman *et al.* 1985; Wasserman *et al.* 1973). The latter group of investigators related the concept of anaerobic threshold to cell redox. Their concept states that at certain intensity lactate increases in the cell because of the mitochondrial proton shuttle. This normally oxidises cytosolic NADH + H^+ as it transfers protons and electrons to mitochondrial O_2, and is too slow to reoxidise the reduced cytosol NAD. This process results in the faster conversion of pyruvate to lactate leading to lactate accumulation.

2) Mass action: When glycolysis proceeds at a faster rate than pyruvate can be utilised by the mitochondrial tricarboxylic acid cycle. This results in elevated pyruvate levels in the cytosol, and consequently lactate accumulation by mass action (Spriet *et al.* 2000).

3) Imbalance between lactate production and removal. Brooks *et al.* (2005) demonstrated that the majority of lactate formed by muscle contraction is not converted to glycogen in the skeletal muscle but oxidised by a variety of tissues

including skeletal muscle, heart muscle, and possibly other organs. Rather than causing oxygen debt, Brooks *et al.* (2005) suggest this process actually pays it off.

4) Contributing factors such as increased catecholamine hormones which increase glycolytic rate, and also the increased recruitment of fast twitch glycolytic motor units (Xu and Rhodes 1999).

1.1.2.2. Enzymatic regulation of Glycolysis:

Lactate is the product of glycolysis as a function of carbohydrate metabolism. During aerobic metabolism, carbohydrates are metabolised through the process of glycolysis, the Tri-Carboxylic-Acid (TCA) cycle, and the electron transport chain to yield 38 moles of ATP for every mole of glucose metabolised. The overall reaction of glucose conversion into lactate is:

Glucose + 2Pi + 2ADP→ 2 lactate + 2 ATP + 2 H_2O

Lactate is produced from pyruvate and NADH via the catalytic reaction of the near equilibrium enzyme lactate dehydrogenase (LDH):

$$LDH$$

Pyruvate + NADH$^-$ → Lactate + NAD$^+$

The glycolytic flux and the increased demands of ATP are known to be affected by exercise intensity. Spriet *et al.* (2000) stated that the higher the demand of ATP, the higher the activation of the glycolytic enzymes. These enzymes can be classified into the following:

a) Non-equilibrium enzymes: Glycogen Phosphorylase, Phosphofructokinase, and to a smaller extent Hexokinase. These enzymes are covalently and allosterically regulated by factors related to intensity of the muscle contraction and the demand of ATP (hormones, Ca^{+2}, muscle ATP, free ADP, AMP, Pi, and H$^+$) (Spriet *et al.* 2000).

b) Near equilibrium enzyme (LDH): Tetrameric enzyme that is not allosterically controlled. LDH has 2 types of subunits, M type in skeletal muscle and liver, and H type mainly in the heart. The M4 isozyme converts pyruvate into lactate to allow glycolysis to proceed, while the H4 isozyme is designed to oxidise lactate to pyruvate. Unlike the M4, the H4 is allosterically inhibited by high level of pyruvate. Thus, LDH is sensitive to the level of its substrates (pyruvate and NADH). According to Bergman *et al.* (1999) LDH is abundant in the cytoplasm, but has been found in the mitochondria along with protein monocarboxylate transporter 1 (MCT-

5

1), and believed to account for mitochondrial oxidation of lactate by variety of cells and tissues (intracellular lactate shuttle). LDH has a large equilibrium constant (about 104), with the lactate to pyruvate concentration ratio in arterial blood is at least 10 in resting humans (Henderson *et al.* 2004). LDH has the greatest catalytic activity of any glycolytic enzyme. It exceeds by many times the combined catalytic activities of enzymes which provide alternative pathways for pyruvate metabolism (Henderson *et al.* 2004) . Thus the balance between lactate and pyruvate interconversion strongly favours lactate in vivo.

With pyruvate availability in muscle, lactic acid will be always formed from pyruvic acid. Therefore, lactate is always an integral part of carbohydrate metabolism. At submaximal exercise intensity, pyruvate concentration found in muscle is sufficient to support maximal catalytic activity of LDH (Brooks *et al.* 1985), and thereby, lactate formation (Figure1.1).

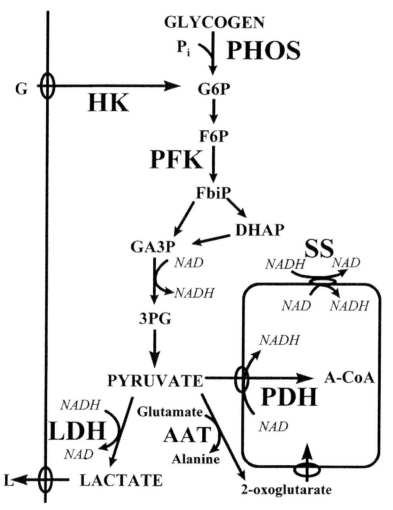

Figure 1.1. Schematic of the glycogenolytic/glycolytic pathways highlighting key enzymes and major routes of pyruvate. The vertical line indicates the muscle membrane separating blood and muscle cytoplasm, the rectangle depicts the mitochondrion, the ellipses indicate a transport process, and the arrows indicate the direction of net flux. G = glucose; L = lactate; A-CoA = acetyl-coenzyme A; PHOS = glycogen phosphorylase; HK = hexokinase; PFK = phosphofructokinase; SS = malate-aspartate shuttle system; LDH = lactate dehydrogenase, AAT = alanine amino transferase; PDH = pyruvate dehydrogenase. Flux through PHOS, HK, and PFK involves a 6-carbon moiety and through SS, PDH, and LDH involves a 3-carbon moiety. Therefore, the metabolism of a 6-carbon glucosyl unit may result in up to a 2-fold higher flux through SS, PDH, and LDH. Extracted from Spriet et al. (1999).

When exercise intensity increases lactate is elevated in both muscle and blood. As intensity increases further, the rate of lactate appearance exceeds the rate of disappearance causing lactate accumulation. Further increases in intensity and corresponding lactate accumulation elevates protons (H^+), where acidosis occur, leading to the termination of exercise.

Lactate is used as a substrate for ATP production, via its conversion to pyruvate, and serves in distributing carbohydrates for oxidation, and gluconeogenesis (Brooks, 1998). Lactate is mainly oxidised when is transported from cytosol into the mitochondria intra- and inter-cellulary, and between active and inactive muscles, which serves a key step in the regulation of intermediary metabolism during sustained exercise (Brooks, 1998). This lactate shuttling enables glycolysis in one cell to supply other cells with fuel for oxidation.

1.1.2.3. Lactate measurements (arterial, venous, capillary):

Differences between arterial and venous lactate must be considered when measuring lactate concentration, and also fitting lactate-intensity curves. Venous blood lactate has been suggested to represent only 60-70% of whole blood lactate (Boning, 2001). It has been demonstrated that arterial blood lactate was higher than the venous blood lactate for the whole lactate-intensity curve, specific lactate thresholds, and different fittings curves, at the same exercise intensity of % $\dot{V}O_{2peak}$ (Robergs *et al.* 1990). This has been attributed to either lactate uptake, or blood flow redistribution through non-exercised muscles.

Capillary blood method is often used in exercise testing by taking blood samples from the finger tip or earlobe. The latter is preferred by some laboratories especially during cycling exercise where hands are in use. Capillary sampling method has been reported to be a good representative of whole body blood lactate (Langlands and Wallace, 1965; cited in Robergs *et al.*, 1991).

1.1.2.4. Gluconeogenesis does not contribute significantly to lactate disposal during exercise:

There are many biochemical factors to justify why gluconeogenesis contribution is of little importance on the lactate fate during exercise. First, it is known that glycolysis and gluconeogenesis are reciprocally regulated. Although both processes are exergonic under cellular conditions, the amount and activities of the distinctive enzymes of each pathway are controlled, so both pathways are not highly active at the same time. For example, the

8

inter-conversion of fructose 6-phosphate and fructose 1,6 biphosphate are strongly controlled by the level of AMP and ATP. While high levels of AMP signal the need for ATP generation, high levels of ATP and citrate indicate that biosynthetic intermediates are abundant. Furthermore, phosphofructokinase and fructose 1,6 biphosphatase are also reciprocally controlled by fructose 2,6-biphosphatase in the liver. Fructose 2,6-biphosphatase stimulates phosphofructokinase and inhibit fructose 1,6-biphosphatse. Thus, glycolysis is accelerated and gluconeogenesis is slowed down in the fed state.

Secondly, it has been shown that the equilibrium between lactate and pyruvate is not affected by their irreversible removal via gluconeogenesis (Henderson *et al.* 2004). The latter group stated that, at moderate and heavy exercise intensities, the rate of lactate to pyruvate conversion is equal to the rate of pyruvate to lactate conversion, and that the rate of pyruvate net release is similar to the rate of lactate net release, with alanin release being relatively small. Henderson *et al.* (2004) concluded that during exercise the rate of inter-conversion between lactate and pyruvate is far greater than the rate of the irreversible removal from blood of lactate and pyruvate i.e. gluconeogenesis.

It is established in literature that lactate clearance during exercise is primarily through increasing oxidation (Donovan and Brooks 1983; Brooks and Gaesser 1980; Henderson *et al.* 2004; Bergman *et al.* 1999). Bergman and Brooks (1999) demonstrated that endurance training increases, both intramuscular and whole body, lactate clearance predominantly through oxidation, with 70 - 80% of the lactate oxidised respectively. Active muscles accounted for 70% of the lactate oxidised and other tissues such as the liver and inactive skeletal muscles accounted for the remaining. Furthermore, Donavan and Brooks (1983) reported lactate oxidation rate of 70-80% of lactate clearance during and after exercise. Similarly, Mazzeo *et al.* (1986) in (Bergman and Brooks 1999), using [L-^{13}C] lactate in exercising humans, reported 82% oxidation rate of lactate disappearance at 50%VO_{2max}, and 78% at 75%VO_{2max}. Therefore, gluconeogenesis contributes very little to lactate disposal during different exercise intensities, and lactate oxidation is the major fate of whole body lactate disposal. Earlier studies on liver metabolism also showed that the liver produces lactate during exercise (Wasserman *et al.* 1987), which diminishes any possibility of glyconeogenesis being highly activated. The ratio between lactate and pyruvate is not affected by glyconeogenesis, thereby will not affect the validity of lactate as an indicator of pyruvate availability during exercise.

1.1.3. Effects of exercise intensity on the utilisation of fat and carbohydrate:

Fat and CHO are the principle substrates that fuel human skeletal muscles at rest and during exercise. The energy from fat and CHO is used for muscle contraction for ATP regeneration. Although protein is a viable source of energy, it is not used to fuel the energy needs of the body at any appreciable extent, except during starvation. The contribution of the oxidation of some amino acids, such as branched chain amino acids and leucine, contribute to sustaining endurance exercise, and may be increased by training (Brooks 1987 in Brooks and Mercier 1994). However, the overall energy flux rates change little, suggesting that fat and CHO are the predominant fuels during exercise (Henderson *et al.* 1985; Brooks 1987; Rennie *et al.* 1994; in Brooks and Mercier 1994).

It is well documented that the relative utilisation of fat and CHO can vary enormously and depends on many factors such as dietary and nutritional status (Bergman and Brooks 1999), exercise mode (Kang *et al.* 2004), intensity and duration (Romijn *et al.* 1993), training status (Coyle *et al.* 1997) and hormonal milieu (Winder *et al.* 1979 in Ranallo and Rhodes 1998). However, exercise intensity appears to be the main factor that relates to all of the latter effects (Achten *et al.* 2002).

Exercise intensity affects storage and the relative use of fat and CHO. Fat utilisation during exercise tends to be highest at low exercise intensities, and declines gradually coupled with a gradual increase in CHO utilisation as exercise intensity increases. Exercise intensities between 30-65 % $\dot{V}O_{2peak}$ tend to elicit the highest fat utilisation, and higher intensities of approximately 85 % $\dot{V}O_{2peak}$ tend to elicit minimal fat oxidation, and almost total dependence on CHO utilisation (Spriet 2002; Romijn *et al.* 1993; Brooks and Mercier 1994; Achten and Jeukendrup 2003; Gonzalez-Haro *et al.* 2007).

Romijn *et al.* (1993) showed that plasma Free Fatty Acids (FFAs) turnover accounts for the fats metabolised during low exercise intensities between 25 - 40 % $\dot{V}O_{2max}$. However, muscle triglycerides contribution increases as the contribution of plasma FFAs slightly decreases at intensity of 65 % $\dot{V}O_{2max}$. At higher exercise intensities such as 85 % $\dot{V}O_{2peak}$ total fat oxidation decreases as well as plasma FFA sources allowing increases in energy sources of CHO (glycogen and glucose).

10

Thus, FFAs utilisation depends on exercise intensity. Plasma FFAs are able to supply most substrate at low intensities, but a limited substrate source at higher intensities. It has not yet been established why the use of FFAs is restricted at those exercise intensities. However, below is a summary of the most viable explanations.

1.1.3.1. The possible mechanisms of the decline in fat metabolism in favour of carbohydrate metabolism:

a)   Fat regulates carbohydrate metabolism:

It has been proposed that the reduction in muscle carbohydrate oxidation rate was caused by high plasma FFA in resting muscles (Randle *et al.* 1963 in van Loon *et al.* 2001). The latter concept related the increased availability of plasma FFAs to suppressing pyruvate dehydrogenase complex (PDH) activation, via rise in mitochondrial acetyle-CoA/CoA ratio, and by decreasing glycolytic flux, via the inhibitory effects of high citrate concentrations on phosphofructokinase activity. Therefore, this concept suggests that the relative utilisation of fat and CHO is determined by the availability of plasma FFAs. However, later studies did not find any connection between FFA availability and the reduction in fat oxidation at high intensity exercise (Romijn *et al.* 1993; van Loon *et al.* 2001).

b)   Carbohydrate regulates fat metabolism:

It has been shown in isolated, contracted and perfused muscles that high CHO availability is associated with reduced long chain fatty acid (LCFA) oxidation (Hargreaves and Spriet 2006). The latter researchers reported several studies in rodent and human muscles suggesting that high CHO availability decreases LCFA oxidation (Dyke *et al.* 2001; Sidossis *et al.* 1997; Turcotte *et al.* 2002, in Hargreaves and Spriet 2006), though this was not observed elsewhere (Yee *et al.* 2001 in Hargreaves and Spriet 2006). In contrast, low CHO availability impair muscle oxidative metabolism because the shift to oxidise fat as the predominant fuel either reduces the production rate of acetyl-CoA or results in an inability to maintain an adequate level of Krebs cycle intermediates. Thus, CHO availability plays an important role in regulating fat oxidation.

Some suggested that increased glycolytic flux rate can directly inhibit FFAs oxidation by either phosphorylating it by its AMP activated kinase (Winder 2001), or by glucose inhibitory effects on LCFA (Coyle *et al.* 1997). It has been suggested that the cellular mechanism for the decrease in LCFA oxidation at rest is linked to an increase in the

11

glycolytic flux and to a subsequent increase in levels of malonyl-CoA (Ruderman *et al.* 1999, Turcotte *et al.* 2002 in Hargreaves and Spriet 2006). High levels of malonyl-CoA inhibit carnitine palmitoyltrasferase-I (CPT-I) activity in the cytosol which limits the FFA entry into the mitochondria, and reduces LCFA oxidation (McGarry *et al.* 1983). Therefore, it has been suggested that high glycolytic flux rates during high intensity exercise indirectly limit LCFA causing down-regulation of CPT-I (Saggerson 1981, in Starritt *et al.* 2000; Van Loon *et al.* 2001). However, the role of malonyl-CoA in inhibiting CPT-I has been questioned in human studies during exercise (Odland *et al.* 1998).

Many factors can determine the level of CPT-1, among which Acetyl-CoA/ CoA (Constantin-Teodosiu *et al.* 1998), reduction in pH (Starritt *et al.* 2000), or the decline in the free carnitine due to increased acetylation (increased acetyle-carnitine) (van Loon *et al.* 2001). Starritt *et al.* (2000) explained that the accumulations of acetyl-CoA, free co-enzyme A, and acetylcarnitine do not counteract the malonyl-CoA induced inhibition of CPT I activity, and small decreases in pH produce large reductions in the activity of CPT I and may contribute to the decrease in fat metabolism that occurs during moderate and intense aerobic exercise intensities. Thus, the current knowledge suggests that the inhibition of CPT-I is due to either decline in free carnitine pool, or a decrease in intracellular pH (van Loon *et al.* 2001).

Increased exercise intensity increases catecholamine hormones causing higher glycolytic flux, and increased CHO oxidation (Brooks and Mercier 1994). The increase in the glycolytic flux is also associated by lactate accumulation. It has been shown that lactate, pyruvate, or both, can directly inhibit lipolysis (Boyd *et al.* 1974).

An increased availability of pyruvate increases has been suggested to be an important trigger for PDH activation among others such as Ca^{+2} concentration, NAHAD/NAD, ATP/ADP, and acetyl-CoA-Co ratios, leading to increased CHO oxidation (Spriet and Heigenhauser 2002). On the other hand, a reduction in pyruvate availability has been associated with reduced CHO oxidation (Mourtazakis *et al.* 2006). Thus, it may be considered that CHO availability can directly or indirectly determine the rate of fat oxidation and regulate the fuel interaction during exercise.

1.1.3.2. Methods of estimating fat and carbohydrate metabolism:

Depending on the aim of the measurements, whether whole body estimation or local muscle substrates, researchers used different methods. These methods are sometimes used in combination to reconcile the estimation of fat and CHO, or to specify the cell compartments and substrate exchange.

1) Muscle biopsy: This invasive method is based on a direct needle biopsy sampling of working muscle as described in Bergstrom (1975). It has been used to directly estimate enzymes controlling fat and CHO oxidation (Odland *et al.* 1998). However, it is unpleasant for subjects, and only represents local muscle substrate (Nordby *et al.* 2006).

2) Stable Tracer Isotopes: This method depends on the rate of appearance and disappearance of radioactive isotopes of ^{14}C, and ^{11}C; or non-radioactive ^{12}C, and ^{13}C. ^{13}C detected by their mass, and has become popular in human experiments (Brooks *et al.* 2005). Recently, new stable isotope methods using heavy water ($^{2}H_2O$) have been used for measurement of both of synthesis of fatty acids (rate of lipogenesis), and triglycerides as important factors in fat accumulation, and the efficiency of production in vivo, in animals, and humans over prolonged periods (Murphy 2006). Isotopes of hydrogen (deuterium ^{2}H, and tritium ^{3}H) have also been used (Brooks *et al.* 2005). Tracers can also assess FFA, and glucose use by measuring of arterio-venous concentration difference across working legs (Friedlander *et al.* 1999). These methods provide specific information on the local muscle, and cellular relative contribution of CHO and fat oxidation, and have been shown to be reliable in comparison to muscle biopsy during several exercise intensities (van Loon *et al.* 2001).

3) Estimation of total body fat and CHO oxidation using indirect calorimetry as described next.

1.1.3.3. The principle of indirect calorimetry:

Indirect calorimetry is known to be a good tool to non-invasively determine substrate utilisation in terms of fat and CHO. This method has been shown to be valid and reliable in comparison to stable isotope trace, and muscle biopsy methods at various exercise intensities (Romijn *et al.* 1993; van Loon *et al.* 2001).

Based on measures of the ratio of CO_2 produced in relation to O_2 consumed it is possible to obtain measures of the mixture of fuels being oxidised under different conditions i.e. at rest and during exercise.

Jeukendrup and Wallis (2005) explained that the stoichiometry for glucose is: $C_6H_{12}O_6 + 6 O_2 \rightarrow 6 CO_2 + 6 H_2O$

A complete oxidation of 1 mole of glucose requires 6 moles of O_2, and produces 6 moles of CO_2. Therefore, the RQ for glucose is 1.

The stoichiometry of palmitic acid is: $C_{16}H_{32}O_2 + 23 O_2 \rightarrow 16 CO_2 + 16 H_2O$

If 1 mol of palmitic acid is completely oxidised it will require 23 moles of O_2 and produce 16 moles of CO_2. The RQ for palmitic acid is 16 / 23 = 0.7. Thus, the relative rates of CHO and fat are estimated between RQ of 0.7-1.

An average amino acid requires 5.1 moles of O_2 and produces 4.1 moles of CO_2. The RQ of protein is therefore 92/114 = 0.807.

Indirect calorimetry reflects the amount of oxygen required to oxidise food stuff (CHO, fat, and protein), and produce carbon dioxide. It depends on the estimation of respiratory quotient (RQ) at the tissue level. Respiratory exchange ratio (RER) reflects the latter gas exchange at lungs and is often used to reflect non-protein RQ (Brooks 1987 in Bergman and Brooks 1999). Jeukendrup and Wallis (2005) explained that protein is broken down into amino acids and deaminated before it is oxidised. Nitrogen and sulphur are exerted in urine, sweat, and feces, and the remaining keto-acid will be oxidised to CO_2 and H_2O in a similar manner to CHO and fat. Measuring protein oxidation requires measuring nitrogenous exertions. However, protein oxidation has been shown to contribute minimally during exercise, and this may only cause an insignificant error that researchers accept for necessity and convenience (Brooks 1987 in Brooks and Mercier, 1994, Brooks et al. 2005).

Therefore, most of the recently reported exercise metabolism studies (Achten and Jeukendrup 2004, Venables et al. 2005, Bircher et al. 2005, Gonzalez-Haro 2007, Burn et al. 2007) opted to use equations that are based on estimating CHO and fat combustion and neglecting protein oxidation. Several equations have been listed in Jeukendrup and Wallis (2005). However, the mostly used equation is (Peronnet and Massicotte 1991):

CHO combustion equation: $4.585 \times \dot{V}CO_2 - 3.226 \times \dot{V}O_2$

Fat combustion equation: $1.695 \times \dot{V}O_2 - 1.701 \times \dot{V}CO_2$

Jeukendrup and Wallis (2005) explained that while $\dot{V}O_2$ reliably reflect tissue O_2 uptake, $\dot{V}CO_2$ is only reliable estimate of tissue CO_2 at low exercise intensities where a stable bicarbonate pool $[HCO_3^-]$ is present. However, this is unlikely in higher exercise intensities when lactate accumulates and hydrogen ions (H^+) increase in muscles and blood. The increased H^+ will be buffered by $[HCO_3^-]$ and a non-oxidative CO_2 is exerted through hyperpnea. This causes elevated $\dot{V}CO_2$ and therefore overestimating CHO and underestimating fat oxidation. Therefore, indirect calorimetry is only reliable when RQ $\leq$ 1. During exercise, this will correspond to exercise intensities of approximately 85 % $\dot{V}O_{2peak}$ (Romijn *et al.* 1993).

1.2. THE INTERRELATIONSHIP BETWEEN LACTATE AND THE RELATIVE RATE OF PYRUVATE COMBUSTION

An interrelationship between lactate accumulation and the substrate oxidation of fat and CHO has previously been reported (Boyd *et al.* 1974; Coggan *et al.* 1992; Achten and Jeukendrup 2004). During exercise CHO, provided by glucose and glycogen, is metabolised in the cytoplasm of skeletal muscle cells to produce pyruvate via the glycolytic pathway. Once produced, pyruvate can be further metabolised in the cytoplasm, via its conversion to lactate, or transported across the inner mitochondrial membrane and metabolised inside the mitochondria. Pyruvate's two fates are summarised as: 1) when transported into the mitochondria the non-equilibrium enzyme pyruvate dehydrogenase (PDH) regulates pyruvate conversion to acetyle coenzyme A (acetyl-CoA) in its irreversible reaction; and 2) when glycolytic rate increases, pyruvate reacts with the near equilibrium nature of lactate dehydrogenase (LDH) to form lactate.

It is important to note that pyruvate has other reactions in the cytoplasm and in the mitochondria which do not contribute significantly to its fate. Pyruvate can combine with glutamate to form 2-oxoglutarate and alanine in the alanine aminotransferase reaction, but this reaction only accounts for about 2-5% of pyruvate disposal (Spriet *et al.* 2000). Furthermore, neither of the reactions catalysed by pyruvate carboxylase nor malic enzyme in the cytoplasm appears to be quantitatively important (Spriet *et al.* 2000). Therefore, the most important pathway of pyruvate is its conversion into lactate. To date, no study used this enzymatic link between pyruvate and BLC as an indicator for substrate utilisation in exercise testing.

1.2.1. Pyruvate availability, lactate and carbohydrate combustion:

Lactate production depends directly or indirectly on the availability of its substrate pyruvate. The increased availability of pyruvate and NADH increases the flux through LDH. When glycolysis is slow LDH competes with the mitochondria for pyruvate, and the near-equilibrium reaction always favours lactate. Pyruvate is one of the major activators of the non-equilibrium enzyme PDH whose activation is relative to the increase in exercise intensity (Howlett *et al.* 1998). Among several factors such as Ca^{+2} and free ADP, pyruvate is the only substrate considered to play both roles of activating PDH allosterically by inhibiting PDH kinase (Wieland 1983), and stimulating flux as a substrate (Spriet and Heigenhauser 2002). This was strongly supported during prolonged moderate exercise, as recently (Mourtzakis *et al.* 2006) who suggested that reduced pyruvate availability has primarily accounted for the reduction in CHO oxidation and ultimately a reduction in PDH activity during continuous cycling at 44% of subjects' $\dot{V}O_{2peak}$. Therefore, pyruvate availability appears to be a regulating factor for the rate of CHO oxidation, and contribute to how much lactate is produced at different exercise intensities.

Spriet et al. (2000) explained the importance of pyruvate availability in regulating the near-equilibrium reaction of LDH as exercise intensity increases. Increased exercise intensities lead to increased pyruvate availability through increased glycolytic flux, which will increase the flux through the near-equilibrium reaction catalyzed by LDH and alanine amino transferase (AAT). This in turn helps to transform PDH to its active form, suggesting that the rate of pyruvate combustion is strongly linked with the level of lactate produced. Thus, a direct estimation or indirect measure of pyruvate availability may be a good indicator for CHO combustion. Lactate measurements may provide a good indication for the relative rate of pyruvate combustion.

One might consider that the activation of PDH, in its irreversible reaction, might not be influenced by pyruvate availability in prolonged moderate exercise intensity over 2 hours. It has been demonstrated that, at the end of a prolonged exercise bout PDH kinase (PDK) activity was elevated and coupled with reduced PDH activity, with no changes in muscle pyruvate and cellular status at the end of 4 hours of continuous exercise at 55% $\dot{V}O_{2peak}$, suggesting that muscle pyruvate was not changed in spite of reduced PDH activity (Watt et al. 2004). However, this was contradicted by later findings (Mourtzakis et al. 2006) who reported that reduced pyruvate availability was associated with a reduction of approximately 13% in CHO after 1 hour of prolonged exercise at 44% $\dot{V}O_{2peak}$.

It has also been reported that pyruvate did not activate PDH in cases for anaplerosis by increasing the tricarboxylic acid intermediates cycle (Constantin-Teodosiu et al. 1999), and also in a glycogen depleted status (Constantin-Teodosiu et al. 2004). However, the latter induced alterations to the Tricarboxylic Acid (TCA) cycle or glycogen availability do not necessarily eliminate the activating role of pyruvate availability. It seems that when pyruvate is available (i.e. non-depleted glycogen status), it contributes to PDH activation, which is in line with the suggestion that CHO availability controls fat metabolism (Coyle et al. 1997, Hargreaves and Spriet 2006).

1.2.2. The interaction between lactate, CHO, and fat during exercise:

1.2.2.1.   General understanding and practical relevance:

Understanding of the mechanisms of fat and CHO interaction during different exercise intensities is very important for health and exercise performance. It has been shown that fuel selection abnormality is associated with metabolic diseases like type-2 diabetes, and obesity (Kelly and Simoneau 1994; Martin *et al.* 1995; Colberg *et al.* 1995, in van Loon *et al.* 2001). Furthermore, it has been suggested that a reduced capacity to oxidise fat is an important factor in developing obesity and type-2 diabetes. This was investigated in Pima Indians who showed higher rate of weight gain due to an elevated 24-h RQ (Zurlo *et al.* 1990 in Jeukendrup and Wallis 2005). The latter subjects have been reported more prone to obesity and type-2 diabetes associated with reduced capacity to oxidise fat, and insulin resistance, because of a change in their lifestyle into a more Western lifestyle (Kelly and Goodpaster, 2001 in Jeukendrup and Wallis 2005). Perez-Martin *et al.* (2001) reported several studies linking obesity epidemic with insulin resistance leading to a decrease in glucose uptake and utilisation, and in glycogen storage. Furthermore, reduced FFA utilisation in obese subjects and subjects with a risk of obesity has been characterised by: a) decrease in lipoprotein lipase; b) decrease in CPT-I and in citrate synthase, which leads to a reduced FFAs transfer into the mitochondria. Exercise training induces metabolic changes that are favourable for the diagnosis, prevention, and treatment of obesity, and therefore was recommended by clinicians (The House of Common Health Committee, 2004; American Diabetics Association, Basdevant *et al.* 1998 in Perez-Martin *et al.* 2001).

Exercise training is known to induce metabolic changes that improve substrate selection. It has been established that an increased capacity of trained muscles to oxidise blood-borne FFAs and TGs, along with an increased capacity to access intramuscular TGs, results in glycogen sparing and increased exercise endurance capacity (Mole *et al.* 1971; Henriksson and Reitman 1977; Oscai *et al.* 1982; Hollozy and Coyle 1984; Gollnick 1985; in Brooks and Mercier 1994). Glycogen availability and sparing are known to be favourable factors to prolong exercise performance, and glycogen depletion has been implicated in fatigue (Below *et al.* 1995; Hargreaves 2004). The latter summarised that muscle glycogen is an important fuel for contracting skeletal muscle during prolonged strenuous exercise, and its availability has several roles: "resynthesis, excitation-contraction coupling, insulin action and gene transcription may be all dependent on glycogen availability during exercise. For example, low muscle glycogen is associated with: reduced muscle glycogenolysis; increased glucose and non-esterified FFA uptake and protein degradation;

accelerated glycogen resynthesis; impaired excitation-contraction coupling; enhanced insulin action and potentiation of the exercise-induced increases in transcription of metabolic genes".

Brooks and Mercier (1994) reviewed CHO and fat interaction with exercise intensity as they defined the cross over concept as the power output at which energy from CHO predominates over energy from lipids. On the other hand, the exercise intensity that elicit maximal fat oxidation has recently been defined (Achten and Jeukendrup 2003; Venables *et al.* 2005). Since then, "metabolic" training at the cross-point has been suggested to improve performance, and that the ability to improve the power output at the cross-point may improve performance (Brooks and Mercier 1994; Billat *et al.* 2003; Brun *et al.* 2007).

1.2.2.2. Effects of lactate on fat utilisation

It is known that the substrate contribution to the total energy requirements depends on exercise intensity. High lactate levels at increased exercise intensity led to the idea that lactate may have direct inhibitory effects on fat, and increase in CHO through lactate oxidation. A direct effect of lactate on fat has been reported for many years in both vitro, and vivo (Issekutz *et al.* 1975, Boyd *et al.* 1974). Infusion of sodium lactate into male cyclists at 40% $\dot{V}O_{2peak}$ caused a reduction in exercise-induced levels of fatty acids and glycerol, suggesting that lactate has a direct effect on adipose tissue lipolysis (Boyd *et al.* 1974). On the other hand, in exercising dog muscles it has been reported that an increased NADH/NAD ratio caused by lactate formation can synthesise a-glycerolphosphate, which is a precursor of glycerol (Issekutz *et al.* 1975).

However, these inhibitory effects may be due to allosteric factors that accompany lactate increase, and may not be caused by lactate itself. Locally applied lactate into subcutaneous abdominal adipose tissues did not reduce fat mobilisation during exercise (Trudeau *et al.* 1999). Additionally, it has been reported that reduced FFA availability at 55% $\dot{V}O_{2peak}$ exercise has no effect on lactate or pyruvate (Stellingwerff *et al.* 2003). It appears that the pH acidic effects that accompany lactate accumulation can inhibit many lipolytic enzymes (Ranallo and Rhodes 1998). Thus, lactate can be considered to have a direct inhibition on the oxidation of fat.

The previous studies suggest that increased level of lactate accumulation may indicate a progressive reduction in fat oxidation. Achten and Jeukendrup (2004) reported a high correlation between the intensity at maximum fat oxidation and the intensity which correspond to the first rise of BLC (r = 0.65). This intensity has been reported at about 63% $\dot{V}O_{2peak}$ in moderately trained athletes (Achten and Jeukendrup, 2004). Higher exercise intensity showed increased lactate levels coupled with a reduction in fat oxidation. Achten and Jeukendrup (2004) based their association between BLC and fat on the theory that BLC reflects changes in muscle pH fairly accurately, and that a small decrease from 7.0 - 6.8 in muscle pH induce a decrease in the amount of fatty acids oxidised (Starritt *et al.* 2000). This suggests a link between the acidic effects of lactate accumulation as one of the main factors responsible of the inhibition of CPT-I, a key enzyme on FFA metabolism when the glycolytic activity is high.

1.2.2.3. Effects of lactate on carbohydrate utilisation

Lactate plays a central role in CHO metabolism. It has been demonstrated that lactate production and utilisation occurs within and among muscles, and lactate rate of oxidation can represent as much as 25% of whole body carbohydrates (Brooks *et al.* 1985; Brooks 1998; Bergman *et al.* 1999). The interaction between lactate with glucose has previously been described (Miller *et al.* 2002; Pagano *et al.* 1997; Lombardi *et al.* 1999; Vettor *et al.* 1997). It has been shown that glucose oxidation is reduced in rat soleus muscle because of lactate infusion (Pearce and Connett 1980). Miller *et al.* (2002) found that lactate infusion increases lactate oxidation, and reduces glucose oxidation. Their methods involved a combination of lactate [3-^{13}C], and [HCO$_3$], and [6,6-^{2}H$_2$] glucose tracers to estimate the rates of oxidations of both lactate and glucose. Lactate was infused by raising resting lactate up to 4 mmol.l^{-1}. The results of the latter study showed that glucose rates of appearance and disappearance were reduced at 55% $\dot{V}O_{2peak}$; whereas, lactate oxidation and glucose production from lactate were increased. Therefore, estimation of lactate oxidation rates may be combined with glucose and glycolytic rates estimations to give a good representation of the rate of CHO combustion.

It has also been shown that glucose turnover is highly related to lactate levels. Coggan *et al.* (1992), in Brooks and Mercier (1994) described differences in blood glucose kinetics during 90-min of continuous cycling at 55% $\dot{V}O_{2peak}$ between subjects with low and high lactate thresholds. High-threshold subjects were defined as those who experienced a steep rise in blood lactate only in response to relatively high-intensity exercise, whereas, low-threshold subjects where those who responded with a rise in blood lactate at moderate to heavy intensity. The subjects with a low lactate-threshold demonstrated higher blood glucose turnout than those with high-thresholds. That suggested that subjects who have a higher lactate threshold have a higher muscle respiratory activity and oxidise less plasma glucose during exercise. This suggests an association between lactate accumulation and glucose levels.

1.2.3. Methodological aspects in describing the lactate, pyruvate, and their interrelationship during exercise:

The relationship between lactate and pyruvate metabolism at the whole body level has not been studied extensively. Based on the biochemical reaction of the equilibrium between pyruvate and lactate, it has been suggested that lactate increase relative to pyruvate can be used as a measure of the relative importance of these two mechanisms (McGilvery, 1983, in Wasserman 1985). Wasserman *et al.* (1985) employed a bilinear model to describe lactate, pyruvate and lactate to pyruvate ratio for the whole body level. It was found that muscle lactate and pyruvate concentrations increase slightly at low levels of exercise without a change in lactate to pyruvate ratio until a threshold work rate. At this work rate lactate abruptly increased, but not pyruvate (Wasserman *et al.* 1985). These researchers identified a threshold point for lactate and for pyruvate, where pyruvate threshold occurred at a higher work rate than that of lactate, and pyruvate slope was less than lactate in its second component. Their finding was explained by that at a certain intensity pyruvate was not oxidised, Wasserman *et al.* (1985) suggest that pyruvate is actively turned into lactate causing an increase in the lactate to pyruvate ratio. This finding suggests that the level of lactate increase thereby may serve as a good indicator for the non oxidised pyruvate.

The latter bilinear model has been suggested to produce less mathematical extremes (residuals) compared with mono-exponential model, thereby may provide a better description for lactate and pyruvate. Conversely, some have used a mono-exponential model for lactate (Yeh *et al.* 1983, Hughson *et al.* 1987), and also suggested that it provides and provided better residual distribution than a bilinear model (Dennis *et al.* 1992). It is not yet established what mathematical model would best describe an interrelationship between lactate and pyruvate in one system. A sigmoid model linking both lactate and pyruvate has been suggested for this purpose (Beneke 2003).

It is known that a near-equilibrium exists between lactate and pyruvate at cellular level, and that this is expected to remain for the whole body level, because lactate oxidation via its conversion to pyruvate has been shown to be the main fate for lactate clearance during exercise (Brooks *et al.* 2005). The tracer methodology has been used to describe an isotopic equilibrium between lactate and pyruvate (Brooks *et al.* 2005). This was based on estimating the relative isotopic lactate, and pyruvate appearance and disappearance, and based on the assumption that the rate of lactate to pyruvate conversion is equal to the rate of pyruvate to lactate conversion. The isotopic equilibrium has been reported to be near 100% which implies that the rate of the interconversion between lactate and pyruvate is far greater than the rate of the irreversible removal of lactate and pyruvate from blood i.e. gluconeogenesis (Henderson *et al.* 2004). The latter group suggested that a percent isotopic equilibrium provides an index of the magnitude of lactate and pyruvate interconversion vs. irreversible disposal of lactate and pyruvate.

Possible considerations when explaining mechanisms of the rate of lactate and pyruvate accumulation may involve measuring both substrates at different tissue compartments. For example, it has been found that a reduction in the isotopic equilibrium between pyruvate and lactate occurred only in arterial but not in venous blood during prolonged exercise, suggesting that tissues other than muscles (heart, lungs, adipose tissues, liver) may be responsible (Henderson *et al.* 2004). Henderson *et al.* (2004) also observed an increase in lactate to pyruvate ratio (or the equilibrium shift towards lactate). These results have previously been supported for the whole body level using enzymatic techniques (Wasserman *et al.* 1985). A change in the whole body lactate to pyruvate ratio was observed only in arterial blood, though that was only observed at higher exercise intensities in the heavy domain (Wasserman *et al.* 1985). Thus, there seems to be an agreement that the equilibrium between lactate and pyruvate may be altered at different tissue levels especially at high exercise intensities, which must be considered if lactate were to be considered as an indicator of pyruvate combustion.

Describing an interrelationship between lactate and pyruvate or CHO utilisation requires considering whether the substrate measurement represents the whole body or just local part of it. It has been reported that one of the problems in estimating fat and CHO oxidation is that substrate metabolism in different organs of the body is not uniform, and that muscle substrate normally has a higher respiratory quotient than the body as a whole (Wasserman 2002).

Most of recently published studies depended on RER measurements to estimate indirect calorimetry for combustion of CHO and fat during exercise (Jeukendrup and Wallis 2005). However, one must consider that indirect calorimetry assumes that the RER adequately reflects the RQ. RER reflects only the combustion of nutrient mixtures of CHO and fat and neglecting the combustion of protein (Brooks 1987 in Brooks and Mercier 1994, Jeukendrup and Wallis 2005).

1.2.4. Linking indirect calorimetry with BLC measurements:

Indirect calorimetry has been shown to be an excellent tool to measure metabolic responses, and it has been validated for estimation of fat and CHO oxidation for any exercise intensity up to 85% $\dot{V}O_{2peak}$ (Romijn *et al.* 1993). On the other hand, lactate has also been described as a metabolic substrate at different cell compartments, and was directly related to pyruvate (Wasserman *et al.* 1985; Henderson *et al.* 2004). Estimating carbohydrates and fat metabolism using indirect calorimetry has often been described in association with lactate measures (Figure 1.2a, b), (Coyle *et al.* 1988; Bergman and Brooks 1999). However, attempts to link these substrate indicators have always lacked a complementary tool to combine the two measures of lactate and RER.

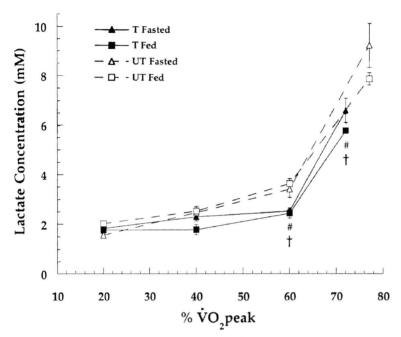

Figure 1.2a. Lactate concentrations (values are means ± SE) for trained (T) and untrained (UT) subjects at 22% (*A*), 40% (*B*), 59% (*C*), and 75% $\dot{V}O_{2\,peak}$ (*D*), as well as mean lactate concentrations (*E*) in fed and fasted states. † Significantly different from UT Fasted, *P* < 0.05; # significantly different from UT Fed, *P* < 0.05. Adapted from Bergman and Brooks (1999).

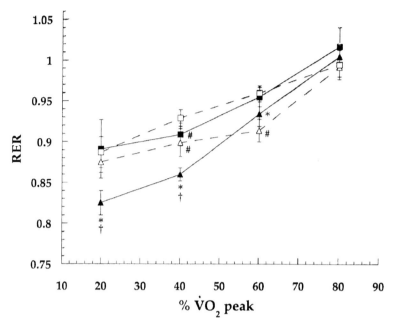

Figure 1.2b. Mean respiratory exchange ratio (RER) values (values are means ± SE) for trained and untrained subjects over time at 22% (A), 40% (B), 59% (C), and 75% (D) $\dot{V}O_{2\ peak}$ in fed and fasted states. E: mean RER values for all time points for trained and untrained subjects in both fed and fasted states. * Significantly different from T fed, $P < 0.05$; † significantly different from UT fasted, $P < 0.05$; # significantly different between UT Fed and UT Fasted, $P < 0.05$. Adapted from Bergman and Brooks (1999).

Brooks and Mercier (1994) indicated that different levels of blood lactate accumulation might indicate intensities for the crossover point, where energy expenditure from CHO predominates over that of fat. However, the latter researchers did not combine their suggestion with experimental testing. Achten and Juekendrup (2004) found an intensity of approximately 63% $\dot{V}O_{2peak}$ corresponds to the intensity at maximum fat oxidation (Fatmax), and 83% for minimum fat oxidation in moderately trained cyclists and triathletes. This corresponded to a BLC of 1.2 and 3.3 mmol.l^{-1} respectively. However, their BLC was unchanged up to the latter intensity, with no significant calculated change in Fatmax for as low as 45% $\dot{V}O_{2peak}$. This was confirmed by their later work (Venables et al. 2005) elicited Fatmax at 47% $\dot{V}O_{2peak}$ lower intensities (Figure 1.3, 1.4), suggesting that a bigger range of BLC may be needed to indicate the high variability in Fatmax intensity.

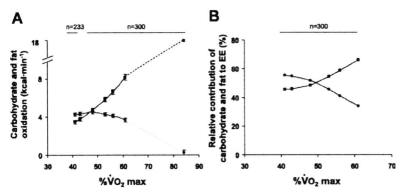

Figure 1.3. Mean absolute (A) and relative (B) substrate energy expenditure at 41, 43, 48, 53, 58, and 61% maximal oxygen uptake ($\dot{V}O_{2\ max}$). n, no. of subjects. ▲, Fat; ■, CHO Extracted from Venables et al. (2005).

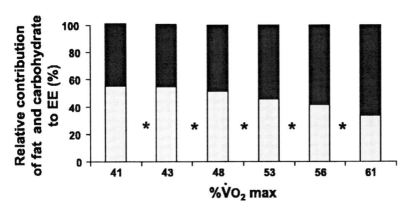

Figure 1.4. Mean relative substrate energy expenditure (EE) at 41, 43, 48, 53, 58, and 61% $\dot{V}O_{2\ peak}$. Values are means; n = 300 subjects. Black bars, CHO; gray bars, fat *Significant difference between adjacent exercise intensities, $P \leq 0.01$. Extracted from Venables et al. (2005).

Wasserman et al. (1985) described the increase in both lactate and pyruvate in a two linear regression model, but have not attempted to estimate or describe the rate of pyruvate or CHO oxidation based on that model. Other polynomial models presented similarities in the response of RER and lactate curves in a descriptive manner such as Bergman and Brooks (1999) who presented increases in RER data to those describing lactate in modifications of fitness level and feeding status (Figures 1.2a, b). Although equilibrium between lactate and pyruvate has been described in different tissue and cell compartments, no investigation has attempted to use lactate as an indicator to measure pyruvate combustion rate for the whole body. Furthermore, literature lacked a complementary model to benefit from this equilibrium. Hence, finding a systematic model linking the BLC with CHO and fat oxidation can be a useful tool to explain the interrelationship between these substrates.

1.2.5. A sigmoid model linking carbohydrate combustion with lactate:
1.2.5.1. Justification:

The behaviour of biological systems is generally nonlinear, which led to the use of exponential functions describing acute physiological responses (Dennis *et al.* 1992; Hughson *et al.* 1987). However, exponential functions are not always sufficient in exercise physiology, especially in describing response delays (Bell *et al.* 1999), or threshold components (Wasserman *et al.* 1990). Sigmoid approximations are able to describe relationships with both nonlinear and relatively linear components such as those seen in the behaviour of many biological sub-systems (i.e. enzyme activation, haemoglobin saturation). Sigmoidality serves as a generalised expression of nonlinear behaviour (Beneke 2003b). Hence, the relative rate of CHO combustion can be described using a sigmoid function of its activator.

When considering lactate as an indicator of pyruvate availability we are assuming an allosteric regulation curve (Berg *et al.* 2002). This curve depends on the allosteric factors (here pyruvate availability), which influence the equilibrium reaction between lactate and pyruvate, and thereby determine the relative rate of pyruvate combustion. These allosteric factors are always sigmodal, and judged by the level of activation by its substrate (Berg *et al.* 2002), which is in this case pyruvate.

Allosteric regulations of the relative rate of pyruvate combustion are affected by the lactate concentration. Therefore, a sigmoid curve can be described by the following steps: 1) There is no, or very little, activation at low pyruvate and lactate levels (and low exercise intensity), this illustrates a flat start of the curve; 2) The activation will increase significantly as pyruvate concentration increases, and also lactate concentration, and this illustrates a steep rise in the curve; and 3) A saturation level will be reached for pyruvate combustion rate even when lactate levels increase. Thus, a sigmoid function may be a good way to describe the relative rate of CHO combustion as a function of lactate accumulation.

1.2.5.2. Description:

BLC increase has been proposed to describe pyruvate dehydrogenase (PDH) activation (Mader and Heck 1986). Their approach was based on a sigmoid curve assuming that

50% of PDH activation takes place at BLC of 4-9 mmol.l^{-1}. The latter researchers took into consideration previous theories and observations relating to steady state lactate concentration, and the elimination of lactate by oxidation, and conversion to glucose (Donovan and Brooks 1983; Issekutz et al. 1975). However, the latter estimated BLC range was based on theoretical assumptions with no experimental proof or BLC measurement.

Beneke (2003b) extended the latter approach to describe linear and nonlinear components of many metabolic systems using sigmoid approximations. His model included a sigmoid relationship between lactate and pyruvate combustion, suggesting a constant of half maximal pyruvate combustion (kel) of 1.8 (mmol.l^{-1})^2. His model included calculating the metabolic power by summing up the rate of glycolysis, oxygen uptake contributing to pyruvate and fat utilisation times their corresponding caloric equivalents, respectively (Equation1.1).

$$\frac{dLa}{dt} = \frac{dLa}{dt}Gly - \frac{dLa}{dt}Ox$$

$$= rM\left(Mu_1 \frac{\frac{dLa}{dt}Glymax}{1+K''\left(\sqrt{\frac{1-Load_1}{K'Load_1}}\right)3} + Mu_2 \frac{\frac{dLa}{dt}Glymax}{1+K''\left(\sqrt{\frac{1-Load_2}{K'Load_2}}\right)3} \right)$$

$$+ (1-rM)\frac{\frac{dLa}{dt}Glymax}{1+K''\left(\sqrt{\frac{1-Load_{nMu}}{K'Load_{nMu}}}\right)3} - \frac{O_2 Equ \dot{V}O_2}{1+\frac{Kel}{La^2}}$$

Equation 1.1. Model describing glycolyis as a function of lactate as developed by Beneke (2003)

dLa/dt is the net glycolytic rate, (dLa/dt)Gly is the glycolytic rate, (dLa/dt)Ox is the rate of pyruvate oxidation, Mu_1 is the mass of primarily engaged muscle, Mu_2 is the mass of assisting muscle, rM is the muscle mass related to body mass, $Load_1$ is the load related to maximum load per unit of primarily engaged muscle, $Load_2$ is the load related to maximum load per unit of assisting muscle, $Load_{nMu}$ is the load related to maximum metabolic load per unit of non-muscular organs, Glymax is the maximum glycolytic rate, K' is the constant of half-maximal activation of cellular performance capacity, K'' is the constant of half-maximal activation of glycolysis, Kel is the constant of half-maximal velocity of pyruvate dehydrogenase, La is the lactate concentration in distribution space, O_2Equ is the lactate oxygen equivalent and $\dot{V}O_2$ is the rate of oxygen uptake. Extracted from (Beneke 2003b)

Equation 1.1 calculates net lactate production as a result of the glycolytic rate and the pyruvate-consumption rate. Net lactate production increases with exercise intensity, fat oxidation compensates for the lack of pyruvate. It considers the relative rate of aerobic pyruvate combustion (RPY) is determined by the availability of pyruvate (Spriet and Heigenhauser 2002), whilst the ratio between lactate and pyruvate is regulated by LDH, which is a near equilibrium enzyme. Therefore, the present work within this book proposes that RPY can be described as a function of BLC. Benefiting from a fraction of the above model (Equation 1.1), the introduced equation would describe RPY as a sigmoid function of BLC as follows:

$$RPY = 100 / (1 + kel / BLC^2)$$

kel is the constant of half maximal pyruvate combustion.

Equation 1.2. Proposed sigmoid interrelationship between BLC and RPY

However, we must take into consideration that the latter proposed interrelationship may be affected by several exercise parameters such as modes, intensity and duration.

1.3. FACTORS AFFECTING THE INTERRELATIONSHIP BETWEEN LACTATE AND RELATIVE PYRUVATE COMBUSTION

1.3.1. EFFECTS OF AVERAGING PERIOD:

Indirect calorimetry isknown to be used for the estimation of CHO and fat oxidation. In incremental exercise testing most researchers based their estimation on averaging almost a whole stage of 2-3 minutes (Achten *et al.* 2002; Achten and Jeukendrup 2003; Achten and Jeukendrup 2004; Venables *et al.* 2005), or at different times of the stage (Bircher *et al.* 2005; Nordby *et al.* 2006; Gonzalez-Haro *et al.* 2007) . This has been prevalent for convenience in obtaining enough data points, or to reducing the noise to signal ratio.

However, the attainment of $\dot{V}O_2$, and $\dot{V}CO_2$ adaptations, especially in incremental testing may require the averaging of a later period of an incremental stage. Differences in fat and CHO estimations were found when the timing of averaging was delayed to a later period (Gonzalez-Haro *et al.* 2007; Bircher *et al.* 2005). The last fraction of an incremental stage, commonly the last 20-30s, is widely used in averaging $\dot{V}O_2$, and $\dot{V}CO_2$ data (Beneke and vonDuvillard 1996; Rossiter *et al.* 2006; Zoladz *et al.* 2002; McDaniel *et al.* 2002). Therefore, if these averaging effects have an impact on respiratory data, one must consider the possible corresponding interrelationship between BLC, and RPY.

1.3.2. DURATION AND INTENSITY OF EXERCISE:

Duration of exercise and the increment size of the test has been shown to play a central role in affecting acute physiological responses of $\dot{V}O_2$ and $\dot{V}CO_2$, BLC, and substrate utilisation of CHO and fat (Beneke 2003c; Jones and Poole 2005; Stockhausen *et al.* 1997; Achten *et al.* 2002). Achten *et al.* (2002) reported no effects on maximum and minimum fat oxidation when the stage duration was reduced from 5 to 3 minutes, or when increment size was reduced from 35 to 20 W. A minimum 2-3 min incremental test protocol is required for the estimation of substrate oxidation of fat and CHO (Jeukendrup and Wallis 2005). Knowing that 3 min may be sufficient for $\dot{V}O_2$ to reach a steady state, one must consider that BLC requires at least 9 -10 min (Stockhausen *et al.* 1997). Establishing a metabolic steady state of BLC requires a long duration, which may last up to 20 min (Beneke 2003b). Furthermore, longer duration has been suggested to be inversely proportional to workload (Stockhausen *et al.* 1997).

Comparisons of different duration protocols from 3-6 min, estimating CHO and fat utilisation using indirect calorimetry, gave different results (Bircher *et al.* 2005; Achten *et al.* 2002). At low exercise intensity the effects seem to be apparent on fat oxidation such as a reduction in Fatmax (Bircher *et al.* 2005). Achten *et al.* (2002) did not find any difference in fat and CHO estimations, at the heavy exercise intensity domain, between 3, 4, and 6 min protocols. However, longer durations at intensity of 65% $\dot{V}O_{2peak}$ showed higher dependence on fat than CHO utilisation compared to an earlier stage, and this was more apparent when glycogen is depleted (Romijn *et al.* 1993). The latter showed that in the first 60 min of this intensity (65%VO_{2max}), plasma FFAs accounted for only 50 - 60% of the total FFAs oxidised but plasma FFAs became the predominant source during prolonged exercise (1-2 hours). Therefore, any interrelationship between BLC-and RPY should consider the latter effects.

Beneke (2003a) developed his model (Equation 1.1) based on a 30-min protocol. He stated that the kel value which links lactate and pyruvate combustion is valid for only prolonged periods of exercise. However, it is not known whether a shorter duration would require a different constant. Thus, further testing of different duration protocol is necessary.

1.3.3. MODES OF EXERCISE:

Different modes of exercise i.e. cycling vs. running, cycling at a low vs. high cadence, with or without handlebar grip have been shown to induce differences on performance and physiological response i.e. BLC, $\dot{V}O_2$, $\dot{V}CO_2$, and power output (Billat *et al.* 2000; Caputo and Denadai 2006; Baker *et al.* 2002). Different muscle mass has been shown to be responsible for differences in BLC induced by different exercise modes (Beneke and vonDuvillard 1996). This was supported by higher BLC when gripping the compared with non-gripping the bicycle handlebar after supramaximal exercise (Baker *et al.* 2002). Muscle contraction frequency and shortening velocity have been reported to be affected by different pedalling rate (Ferguson *et al.* 1999, Zoladz *et al.* 2002). A high pedalling rate increases the frequency of muscle activation and relaxation velocity, compared to a lower rate which leads to higher BLC, $\dot{V}O_2$, and $\dot{V}CO_2$ at both maximal and submaximal exercise intensities (Deschenes *et al.* 2000; Zoladz *et al.* 2002). Different pedalling rates have also been reported to alter the work efficiency which decreases as the pedalling rate increases (Gaesser and Brooks 1975). Contraction frequency has also been attributed to differences in energy expenditure from CHO and fat oxidation for 10 minutes of low intensity cycling (at 50 W) in lower and upper body (Kang et al. 2004).

Changes in pedalling rates induced differences in $\dot{V}O_2$, $\dot{V}CO_2$, which corresponds to changes in the relative rate of substrate utilisation of fat and CHO (Kang et al. 2004). The latter found that CHO oxidation was higher when cycling at 80 rpm compared with 40 rpm at power output of 50 W for 10 min. Similar results were found during an incremental exercise with a cadence of 50 rpm compared with 90 rpm (Hughes et al. 1982). The latter group showed that a higher pedalling rate depleted glycogen quicker than a lower rate, suggesting that might be a reason for fatigue mechanisms.

Pedalling rate and handgrip can be used as examples of modes of exercise. It is known that at high exercise intensity muscular contribution from the upper body muscle mass via the handgrip contributes significantly to the whole body energetics i.e. BLC during the assessment of lower body cycling (Baker et al. 2002). However, it is unknown whether muscle mass contribution, induced by the handgrip will change the relationship between Lactate and CHO combustion, and so require further investigation.

Beneke (2003a) stated that the interrelationship between lactate and the relative rate of pyruvate combustion will not change by changing modes of exercise. He suggested that kel value of 1.8 $(mmol.l^{-1})^2$ will not change in rowing versus cycling exercise. This suggests that the BLC-RPY interrelationship is independent of modes of exercise. However, further investigation is required to find out whether different modes of exercise, such as the pedalling rate and handgrip, affect the BLC-RPY interrelationship.

1.4. RESEARCH QUESTION

Is there a sigmoid interrelationship between BLC and RPY? The present work will test whether and how the BLC-RPY interrelationship is affected during incremental exercise. This work will investigate whether and how the proposed BLC-RPY interrelationship is affected by data processing and averaging or sampling the exercise protocol, and exercise intensity, duration, and modes.

CHAPTER TWO
GENERAL METHODS

2.1. GENERAL:

Subjects who volunteered for this project were briefed as to the benefits and the risk of participation and gave written informed consent to participate in this study, which was approved by the Ethics committee of the University of Essex. Subjects were instructed to avoid any strenuous exercise or alcohol consumption in at least the 24 hours preceding a test session and to arrive at the laboratory in a fully hydrated state, without consuming any heavy meal for at least two hours prior to the test. Subjects consumed the same diet in the day before each test.

2.2. EXPERIMENTAL CONDITIONS:

2.2.1. Environmental Conditions:

Experiments were always performed at the same time of the day and under similar environmental conditions (19 ± 0.8 C, 55 ± 9.1% relative humidity, and 1022 ± 11 mmHg).

2.2.2. Ergometry:

All test protocols were performed on an electromagnetically braked cycle Ergometer (Lode Excalibur Sport, Groningen, The Netherlands). The ergometer's flywheel braking system is controlled using a computer interface. Saddle and handle bar height, handlebar reach, and angle were recorded for the first test and reproduced for the subsequent tests. Saddle height was individually adjusted so that it elicits the maximum power of the lower body as described in Micklewright *et al.* (2006). A toe clip was applied to firmly hold subject's feet with the pedals. The subjects were familiarised with the cycling procedure in a prior visit to the laboratory. For each test, subjects were instructed to remain seated and were given the same level of verbal encouragement throughout the duration of the test. Volitional exhaustion was determined as they could no longer maintain the required pedalling rate for longer than 15 seconds.

2.3. DATA COLLECTION, ANALYSES, AND STATISTICS

2.3.1. Blood Sampling:

Vasodilatation hyperaemic gel (Finalgon, Thomae, Biberach, Germany) was applied on the earlobe, before taking the puncture using manual lancets, at a similar time for all subjects.

Manual sterile disposable lancet was used to penetrate the skin by approximately 2mm. End to end capillary tubes were used to collect 20µl blood samples from the hyperaemic earlobe within a period of approximately 15 s. The capillary tube is then immersed into 1ml of system solution in a sample cup, sealed, and shaken to mix. The system solution is a hypotonic buffer solution (approximately 90 mOsmol.kg^{-1}) of the following composition (Eppendorf Ebio Plus manual):

Disodium hydrogen phosphate	10 mmol.l^{-1}
Potassium dihydrogen phosphate	3 mmol.l^{-1}
(Ethylenedinitrilo) tetracetic acid	
Disodium salt dehydrate	1 mmol.l^{-1}
Dextran 70 for injection ph. Eur. II	2 g.l^{-1}
Sodium fluoride	10 mmol.l^{-1}
Preservative	0.05%
Non-surfactant	0.01%

The sealed samples' cups were loaded into the sample tray, which is then loaded into the lactate analyser. The lactate analyser used was Ebio Plus, Eppindorf, Hamburg, Germany. The samples were analysed for whole blood lactate using amperometric techniques. The coefficient of variation of the latter machine was 0.05 mmol.l^{-1}. This was also tested for repetitive analyses for identical resting samples taken from the same subject at rest, producing a coefficient of variation of 0.06 mmol.l^{-1}.

Before analysing any blood samples, calibration of the machine is performed. This includes measuring 2 and 10 mmol.l^{-1} quality control samples measured using 10 mmol.l^{-1} standard system solution. The machine measures a zero sample before each lactate sample for standardisation. The Lactate analyser operates as follows: samples are presented in closed secondary samples in a tray with 60 positions. Standard and quality controls are presented outside the sample tray.

Lactate is determined with the aid of the enzyme electrode in the analyzer, according to the enzymatic amperomatic principle of measurement as follows: The measuring cycle begins with the immersion of the sample probe into a sample. During this process, sample solution is aspirated into the measuring chamber. The lactate membrane contains the immobilized active enzyme lactate oxidise (LOD). The lactate, which penetrates the measuring chamber during aspiration, encounters the immobilized LOD. This catalyses the oxidation of lactate to pyruvate in accordance with reaction equation (2.1a, b):

$$\text{L-(+)- lactate} + O_2 \xrightarrow{\text{LOD}} \text{Pyruvate} + H_2O_2 \qquad \text{(equation a)}$$

The hydrogen peroxide then formed is oxidized in accordance with reaction equation (2) at the platinum electrode:

$$H_2O_2 \xrightarrow{\text{+600 mV}} 2H^+ + O_2 + 2e^- \qquad \text{(equation b)}$$

Equation 2.1 a,b. Amperometric blood lactate analysis

The measuring signal differentiating continuously during sampling is recorded as the maximum gradient of the differentiated (Current-time curve). The respective measuring signal (maximum of differentiating curve) is converted into a voltage value. This measured value is proportional to the lactate concentration of the sample. After determination of the measured value, the sample is rinsed out of the measuring chamber with system solution.

2.3.2. Respired gas analyses:

The Respiratory gases of oxygen uptake ($\dot{V}O_2$) and carbon dioxide production ($\dot{V}CO_2$), were collected continuously breath by breath throughout each test using an online gas analyser (Oxycon Pro, Jaeger, Hoechberg, Germany). The subject respired through a mouth piece attached to a low- resistance low dead space turbine volume transducer (Triple V turbine, Hans Rudolph, Kansas, USA).

Gas analysers were calibrated online for gas volume and concentration automatically. The volume calibration consisted of measuring the flow values of a two point calibration of 0.2 and 2.0 $l.s^{-1}$. The concentration calibration of O_2 and CO_2 gases was performed using a calibration gas cylinder automatically, and divided into three phases: flushing the tube system; determination of the delay time; and gain settings.

2.3.3. Statistical analyses:

All data analyses and statistics were performed using SPSS statistical software (SPSS release 14.00). The significance level was set at $p < 0.05$.

CHAPTER THREE

RELATIVE RATE OF CARBOHYDRATE COMBUSTION AS A FUNCTION OF BLOOD LACTATE CONCENTRATION

3.1. INTRODUCTION

Indirect calorimetry is known to be a valid and reliable indicator for the estimation of fat and CHO oxidation rates. It has been compared and validated against other measures such as stable isotope tracers (Brooks *et al.* 2005; Romijn *et al.* 1993). Lactate is known to be an indicator of the glycolytic activity since the early twentieth century (Hill *et al.* 1924), and its concentration in blood (BLC) becomes a standard measure of exercise intensity (Beneke 2003b).

Pyruvate results through the breakdown of CHO via glycolysis. Pyruvate has two fates, either aerobically combusted or converted to lactate. The relative rate of aerobic pyruvate or carbohydrate combustion (RPY) is determined by pyruvate dehydrogenase complex (PDH) activity in which pyruvate availability is a key factor among others such as Ca^{+2} concentration, and NADH/NAD, ATP/ADP, acetyl-CoA-Co ratios (Spriet and Heigenhauser 2002), (see chapter 1 for further reading). On the other hand, the ratio between lactate and pyruvate is regulated by the near equilibrium enzyme lactate dehydrogenase (LDH). This ratio is not affected by other pathways of lactate during exercise i.e. gluconeogenesis (Brooks *et al.* 2005), or pyruvate fates i.e. pyruvate combination with glutamate, and pyruvate carboxylase catalytic reaction (Spriet *et al.* 2000), (see chapter one for further details). Consequently, lactate may be useful as an indicator of the relative rate of pyruvate combustion.

Various studies referred indirectly to the interrelationship between lactate measurements and indirect calorimetry (Bergman and Brooks 1999; Achten and Jeukendrup 2004). Billat *et al.* (2004) demonstrated that an average lactate steady state of 4 mmol.l^{-1} corresponded to about 90% CHO combustion and 65% $\dot{V}O_{2peak}$ for endurance runners, suggesting that BLC magnitude can be a useful indicator for interaction points between the combustion of fat and CHO. However, none of the previous studies describe this interrelationship in a joint system.

It has been suggested that whether the blood lactate concentration and its increase reflect the metabolic pattern of working muscles or not, it is justifiable to use its level as an indicator of pyruvate availability, and relative PDH activation (Mader and Heck 1986a; Beneke 2003a; Beneke 2003a; Beneke 2003b).

Describing the interrelationship between lactate and the rate of pyruvate combustion in a model has been paid little attention in literature. Wasserman *et al.* (1985) used a bilinear model to fit lactate, pyruvate and the lactate-pyruvate ratio, though this was opposed by a lactate-describing exponential model proposed by Hughson *et al.* (1987). However, no suggestions were made on the feasibility of such models for the estimation of CHO, or fat combustion rates.

Mader and Heck (1986) were the first to introduce a model describing the rate of PDH activation as a function of BLC assuming that 50% of the level of PDH saturation takes place at BLC of 4-9 mmol.l^{-1}. Their approach was based on a sigmoid curve, suggesting a kel values corresponding to 4-9 (mmol.l^{-1})^2. Those values considered previous theories and observations relating to the lactate steady state, its concentration, and elimination of lactate by oxidation and conversion to glucose (Donovan and Brooks 1983; Issekutz *et al.* 1975 in Mader and Heck 1986). However, this range of kel was based on theoretical assumptions with no experimental proof or BLC measurement.

Beneke (2003b) extended the latter approach to describe linear and nonlinear components of many metabolic systems using sigmoid approximations. His model included a sigmoid relationship between lactate and pyruvate combustion, suggesting a kel 1.8 (mmol.l^{-1})^2. The latter value was approximated to support modelling of experimental data under his conditions. In a later study, Beneke (2003a) extended the understanding of the BLC-RPY by demonstrating the effects of increasing the magnitude of kel on the rate of pyruvate combustion. Approximately 4-5 (mmol.l^{-1})^2 were modelled using computer simulation, but lacked experimental testing.

The purpose of this chapter is to experimentally test the hypothesis of sigmoid interrelationship between lactate and the relative rate of pyruvate combustion. Additionally we propose to test the magnitude of that interrelationship, and whether it correlates with exercise intensities that determine CHO, and fatty acids utilisation, and selected concepts used for exercise testing such as the cross-over point and Fatmax.

3.2. METHODS:

3.2.1. Protocol:

Subjects were 21 healthy males (age: 26.3 ± 6.0 yrs, height: 179.4 ± 8.1 cm, body mass: 74.9 ± 12.5 kg), who completed an incremental load cycling test until exhaustion at 50 rpm. Starting with 1 W.kg^{-1} body mass, power output was increased by 0.5 W.kg^{-1} body mass every 2 minutes. Capillary blood samples were taken from the hyperaemic earlobe at rest and at the end of each stage, and further analysed for whole blood lactate level as described in the general methods (Chapter 2). Respiratory measurements of $\dot{V}O_2$ and $\dot{V}CO_2$ were obtained breath by breath using computerised equipments as described previously (Chapter 2).

3.2.2. Data analyses, modelling, and statistics:

Peak power was calculated from the last completed workload before subjects' exhaustion, plus the time spent in the final non-completed workload multiplied by the work load increment (Achten and Jeukendrup 2003). Relative exercise intensities were defined as a percentage of peak power. Peak and submaximal $\dot{V}O_2$ and $\dot{V}CO_2$ data were averaged for the last 30-s of every stage of the incremental exercise test. RER was calculated as ($\dot{V}CO_2 / \dot{V}O_2$). $\dot{V}O_2$ and $\dot{V}CO_2$ data beyond RER=1 were not used for further analyses.

Pyruvate/CHO combustion was estimated using the stoichiometric indirect calorimetry (CHO = 4.585 * $\dot{V}CO_2$ - 3.226 * $\dot{V}O_2$) as described in Peronnet and Massicotte (1991). Full pyruvate combustion, when $\dot{V}O_2$ equals $\dot{V}CO_2$, was considered to calculate the relative rate of pyruvate combustion (RPY). RPY was then calculated as a percentage of the full pyruvate combustion. RFAT was calculated as 100 - RPY.

The RPY was further approximated as a sigmoid function of lactate RPY = 100 / (1 + kel / BLC^2), (see chapter 1 for further details on the latter equation). Absolute pyruvate and fat combustion rates were calculated based on the O$_2$ required to oxidise glycogen (0.8251 l.g^{-1}), and average fatty acid (C$_{17.2702}$ H$_{32.7142}$ O$_2$), which requires (2.0093 l.g^{-1}), as reported in Jeukendrup and Wallis (2005). Furthermore, maximal fat oxidation rates and the intensities at which it occurred were determined for each individual as described previously

(Achten and Jeukendrup 2003). Energy expenditure (EE) was calculated from the absolute rates of CHO and fat oxidation where EE derived from 1 g is: Fat = 9 kcal, CHO = 4 kcal (1 kcal = 4.184 kJ). The cross over point (cross-point) was calculated as the power output (or exercise intensity) where EE derived from CHO predominates over that of fat (Brooks and Mercier 1994).

The power output, intensity, $\dot{V}O_2$, $\dot{V}CO_2$, BLC, and CHO oxidation were averaged for each incremental stage where all subjects completed that stage. The increase in $\dot{V}O_2$, $\dot{V}CO_2$, BLC, and CHO oxidation was plotted as a function of power output. The magnitude of the increase in $\dot{V}O_2$, $\dot{V}CO_2$, BLC, and CHO was compared between incremental stages.

Linear and nonlinear regression models were used to fit the $\dot{V}O_2$, $\dot{V}CO_2$, and BLC data and describe them at both maximal and submaximal intensities . $\dot{V}O_2$ was fitted using a linear regression model: (y = a * x + b), where x is exercise intensity and y is $\dot{V}O_2$ (McArdle *et al.* 2001), which excluded values at test termination (avoiding the levelling of) (Motulsky and Ransnas 1987). $\dot{V}CO_2$ and BLC data were fitted as a function of exercise intensity using a 3-parameter mono-exponential model: (y = a* e (x * b) + c), where x is exercise intensity, and y is either BLC or $\dot{V}CO_2$ (Alkhatib and Beneke 2005; Dennis *et al.* 1992). All data were described as mean ± standard deviation, minimum / maximum. Between intensity differences were tested using a repeated measures one way ANOVA, with a post hoc Bonferroni test. Correlation coefficients were tested using Pearson's product-moment correlation coefficient.

3.3. RESULTS:

3.3.1. Peak data:

Peak data were (mean ± SD (min/max)), power output 293.3 ± 39.4 (236.3 / 410.0) W, $\dot{V}O_2$ 3885 ± 505 (3305 / 5292) ml.min^{-1}, $\dot{V}CO_2$ 4505 ± 598 (3378 / 6213 ml.min^{-1} and RQ 1.16 ± 0.07 (1.10 / 1.29), and BLC (9.4 ± 2.2 (4.9 / 13.4) mmol.l^{-1}.

3.3.2. Submaximal data:

$\dot{V}O_2$ increased almost linearly as a function of power output by 420.7 ± 57.1 (343.2 / 485.4) ml.min^{-1} per stage equivalent to 11.8 ± 1.8 (9.3 / 14.5) ml.min^{-1}.W^{-1} (Figure 3.1).

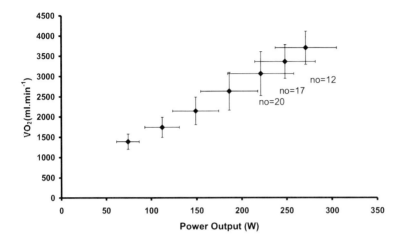

Figure 3.1. The increase of $\dot{V}O_2$ as a function of power output.

$\dot{V}CO_2$ increased ($p < 0.05$) with each increase in power output. Above 149 ± 25 (112 / 212) W the increase in $\dot{V}CO_2$ became progressively steeper ($p < 0.05$) (Figure 3.2).

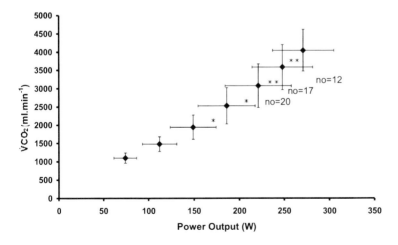

Figure 3.2. $\dot{V}CO_2$ increase as a function of power output. * Significantly steeper than the first stage. ** Significantly steeper than all previous stages but not the one directly preceding.

BLC increased (p < 0.05) with each power output. Above 149 ± 25 (112 / 212) W the increase in BLC became progressively steeper (p < 0.05) (Figure 3.3).

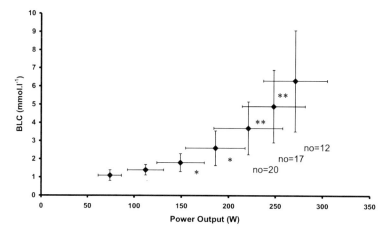

Figure 3.3. BLC increase as a function of power output. * Significantly steeper than the first and second stages. ** Significantly steeper than all previous stages but not the one directly preceded.

CHO oxidation rate increased almost continuously as the workload increased (p < 0.05), (Figure 3.4). However, the increase between 149 ± 25 (112 / 212) and 186 ± 31.6 (140 / 265) was steeper than all other changes in CHO (p < 0.01).

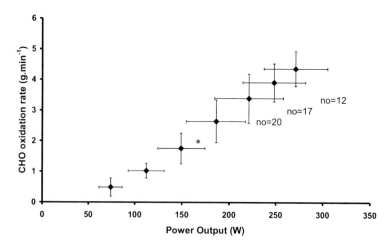

Figure 3.4. Pyruvate oxidation rate increase as a function of power output. * Significantly steeper than the initial stage at the start of the test.

Fat oxidation rate decreased inversely to the increase in CHO oxidation (Figure 3.5). The steepest decrease in fat oxidation was found between 149 ± 25 (112 / 212) and 186 ± 31.6 (140 / 265), (p < 0.01).

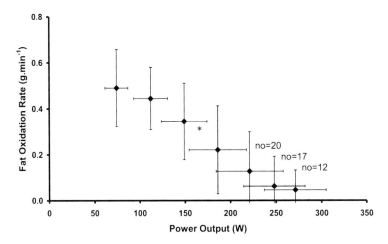

Figure 3.5. Fat oxidation rate decrease as a function of power output. * Significantly steeper decrease than the initial stage at the start of the test.

Describing RPY as a sigmoid function of BLC explained 86 ± 0.09% of the variance in RPY (Figure 3.6). RPY appears more or less saturated at 96.5 ± 8.1% at BLC levels of 4.9 ± 2.0 (1.03 / 6.9) mmol.l^{-1}.

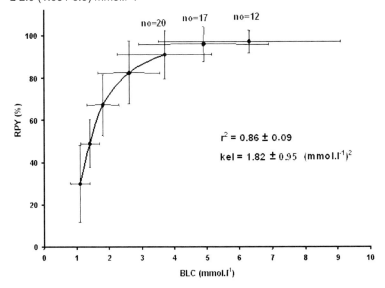

Figure 3.6. Sigmoid interrelationship describing the RPY as a function of BLC. The fitting line was not displayed for the data corresponding to RQ>1

Estimates of kel were 1.82 ± 0.95 $(0.54 / 4.4$ $(mmol.l^{-1})^2$. All individual results are shown in appendix A (Table A1).

Given the above described pattern of increases in $\dot{V}O_2$, $\dot{V}CO_2$ and BLC related to workload, all individual $\dot{V}O_2$ responses were well described as a linear function of intensity related to peak power ($r^2 = 0.992 \pm 0.008$, all $p < 0.001$). $\dot{V}CO_2$ ($r^2 = 0.997 \pm 0.002$, all $p < 0.001$) and BLC ($r^2 = 0.997 \pm 0.005$, all $p < 0.001$) were best described as an exponential function of exercise intensity.

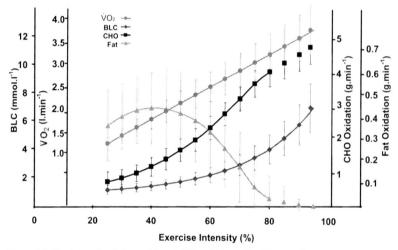

Figure 3.7. The interaction between fat and CHO oxidation with BLC as a function of exercise intensity. Minimum exercise intensities started from 25% where it is elicited in all subjects.

Figure 3.7 illustrates the corresponding intensity dependent behaviours of BLC, $\dot{V}O_2$, CHO and fat oxidation in intensity increments of 5%. RPY reached its saturation level of 100% (RQ =1) at intensity of 86.0 ± 11.8 $(45.0 / 100.0)$ % equivalent to 90.0 ± 12.3 $(51.3 / 100.0)$ % $\dot{V}O_{2peak}$. RPY saturation level also corresponded to BLC levels of 5.6 ± 2.3 $(1.9 / 12.8)$ $mmol.l^{-1}$.

The cross-point where the energy from CHO becomes the predominant fuel source over fat was undetectable in 3 of the 21 subjects due to selecting exercise intensities starting from 25%. In the remaining 18 subjects, the exercise intensity at the cross-point was 38.6 ± 9.5 $(24.7 / 55.0)$ % of peak power, equivalent to 46.1 ± 9.7 $(33.8 / 64.1)$ % $\dot{V}O_{2peak}$, and corresponded to EE from CHO and fat of 4.21 ± 1.13 $(2.82 / 6.51)$ $kcal.min^{-1}$ (Figure 3.8a, b). The cross-point occurred at RPY of 48.2%, corresponding to levels of BLC of 1.3 ± 0.4 (0.8 / 2.1) (Figure 3.8b).

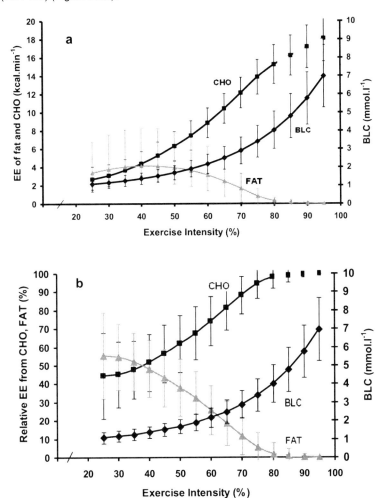

Figure 3.8. The cross-over point between relative (a) and absolute (b) energy expenditure of CHO (■) and fat ( )▲

Fatmax was 0.46 ± 0.17 (0.10 / 0.77) g.min^{-1} corresponded to an intensity of 40.0 ± 9.7 (25.0 / 55.0) % of peak power, which is equivalent to 47.2 ± 9.7 (30.1 / 63.9) % $\dot{V}O_{2peak}$. BLC level at Fatmax was 1.4 ± 0.4 (0.6 / 2.3) mmol.l^{-1} (figure 3.7).

Furthermore, neither the intensity at Fatmax, nor BLC at Fatmax were different from those of the cross-over point. However, EE from Fatmax was higher (p < 0.01) than that at the cross point 4.81 ± 1.1 (3.1 / 7.1) vs. 4.2 ± 1.1 (2.8 / 6.5) Kcal.min^{-1} (no=18).

3.3.3. Correlations:

There was no correlation between kel and relative peak power, $\dot{V}O_2$, $\dot{V}CO_2$, or peak BLC (Figure 3.9a, b, c).

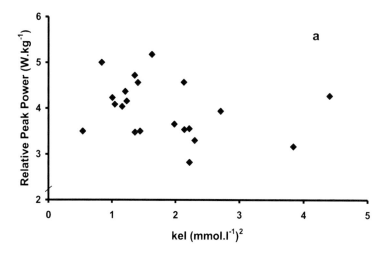

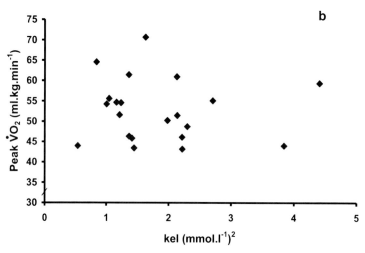

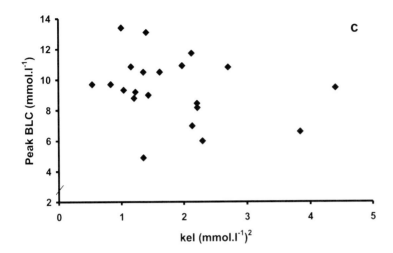

Figure 3.9. No correlation between kel and relative peak power (a), $\dot{V}O_{2peak}$ (b), and peak BLC (c).

Furthermore there were no correlations between kel and relative $\dot{V}O_2$, or power at given submaximal levels of BLC such as 2 and 4 mmol.l^{-1} (Figure 3.10a, b).

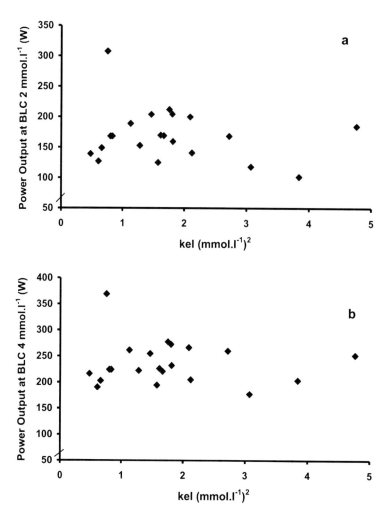

Figure 3.10. (a, b) No correlation between kel and selected BLC thresholds: a) power output at BLC 2 mmol.l^{-1} b) power output at 4 mmol.l^{-1}

The exercise intensity at the cross-over point correlated positively with the magnitude of kel (r = 0.61, p < 0.05), (Figure 3.11).

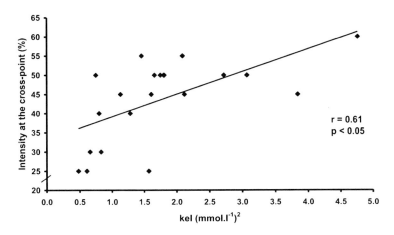

Figure 3.11. Positive correlation between kel and the cross over intensity

The exercise intensities at 90% of RPY (RQ = 0.97) were 78.2 ± 12.7 (48.4 / 96.7) % of peak power, and 81.3 ± 12.9 (54.3 / 107.2) % $\dot{V}O_{2peak}$, corresponding to levels of power output of 230.3 ± 53.3 (139.8 / 339.6) W correlated positively with kel (r= 0.662, p < 0.001), (Figure 3.12).

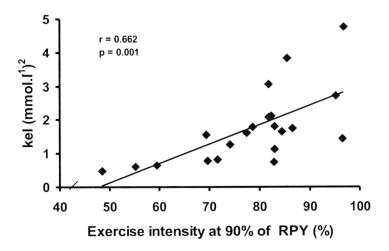

Figure 3.12. Positive correlation between kel and intensity at 90% RPY

Those intensities at 90% of RPY corresponded to BLC levels of 3.8 ± 1.2 (2.1 / 6.5) mmol.l^{-1}. Neither peak power, nor $\dot{V}O_{2peak}$ correlated with the latter intensities, or BLC-levels (Figure 3.13a, b, c, d).

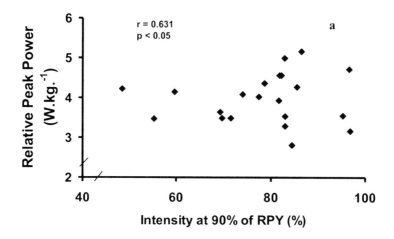

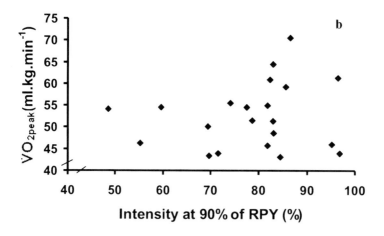

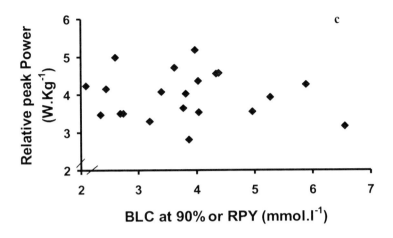

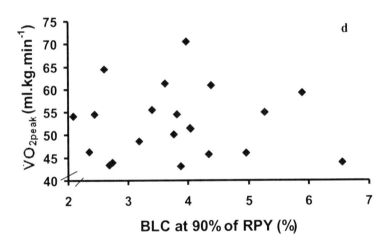

Figure 3.13. No correlation between intensity at 90% of RPY and peak power (a), or peak oxygen uptake (b). No correlation between BLC at 90% of RPY and peak power (c), or peak oxygen uptake (d).

Furthermore, the intensities at 90% of RPY and BLC levels were positively correlated (r = 0.724, p < 0.001) (Figure 3.15).

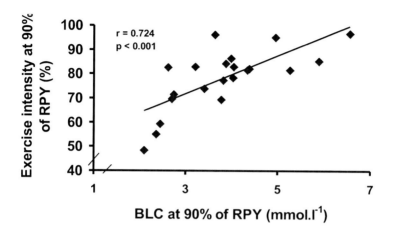

Figure 3.15 Positive correlation between BLC, and exercise intensity at 90% of RPY

Fatmax (r = 0.511, p < 0.05), and the intensity at Fatmax (r = 0.485, p < 0.05), were positively correlated with the magnitude of kel (Figure 3.16, 3.17).

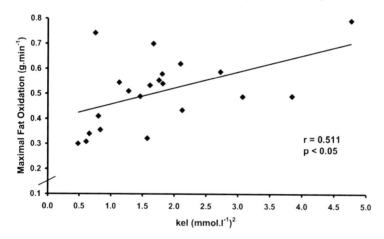

Figure 3.16. Positive correlation between kel and maximal fat oxidation

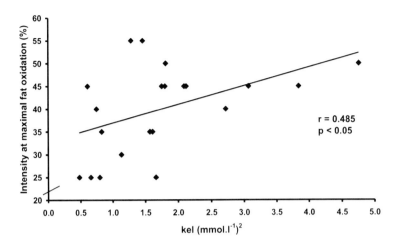

Figure 3.17. Positive correlation between kel and the intensity at maximal fat oxidation

However, maximal fat oxidation was independent of the intensity at Fatmax (Figure 3.18).

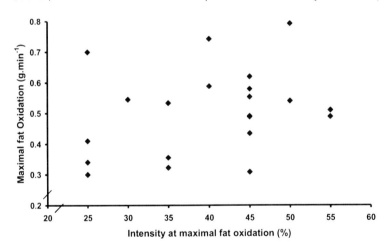

Figure 3.18. No correlation between the maximal fat oxidation and the intensity at which it occurs

3.4. DISCUSSION

The main finding of the present study is that PRY can be described as a function of BLC according to equation 1.1 (Chapter 1). Levels of kel found in the present experiment support assumptions used in most recent modelling (Beneke 2003b). The latter estimated a kel value of 1.8 $(\text{mmol.l}^{-1})^2$ for the simulation of constant workloads in the heavy and severe exercise intensity domains. However, the present results furthermore indicate a high variability in kel values between subjects ranging from $0.54 - 4.4$ $(mmol.l^{-1})^2$.

The present findings show the functional link between BLC, CHO, and fatty acids utilisation, and support previous models such as the cross-over concept (Brooks and Mercier 1994), and confirm theories describing energy metabolism as a function of glycolysis, oxidative rate and lactate availability (Mader and Heck 1986b). They also extend recent findings about exercise conditions at which fatty acid combustion is maximal (Venables *et al.* 2005; Achten and Jeukendrup 2004). Furthermore, the present results seem to support indirectly the high inter-individual variability of BLC at the exercise intensity corresponding to selected concepts of anaerobic threshold and the maximal lactate steady state (Beneke 2003b).

3.4.1. kel and the cross-over point:
The cross-over point is defined as the power output at which energy derived from CHO predominates over that of fat (Brooks and Mercier 1994). The results of this study showed that kel is positively correlated with the intensity at the cross-point (Figure 3.11). This suggests that kel may serve as a useful indicator for the cross-over point and the biochemical adaptations that affect CHO and fat oxidation at that point as explained in Brooks and Mercier (1994). The down regulation of fatty acid oxidation is considered to increase as exercise intensity increases, with CHO metabolism as the main regulator of fat metabolism (Sidossis *et al.* 1997; Coyle *et al.* 1997). Further details about CHO and fat regulation are explained in chapter1.

Our intensity at the cross-point was 46% $\dot{V}O_{2peak}$. This is close to an intensity of 48% $\dot{V}O_{2peak}$ reported in Venables *et al.* (2005), with a similar range of approx. 35 - 65 % $\dot{V}O_{2peak}$. Therefore, inter-individual variability in kel between $0.5 - 4.4$ $(mmol.l^{-1})^2$ may explain the inter-individual variability at the cross-over point as shown in figure 3.19a.

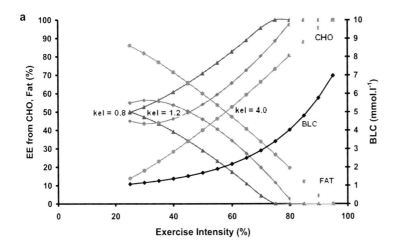

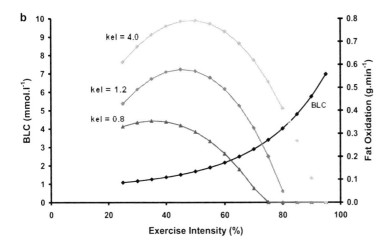

Figure 3.19. Example of the effects of kel variation on the cross-point (a), and the fat oxidation (b). Higher kel induces a shift to the right in the occurrence of Fatmax, and increases the intensity difference between Fatmax and the cross-point.

3.4.2. kel and maximal fat oxidation:

kel was positively correlated with the intensity at maximal fat oxidation (Figure 3.16, 3.17). Similar to previous findings (Achten and Jeukendrup 2004), we observed high inter-individual differences in Fatmax and the intensity at Fatmax. Only few studies (Table 3.1) have corresponded Fatmax to any range of BLC measures (Bircher and Knechtle 2004; Bircher *et al.* 2005; Achten and Jeukendrup 2004; Gonzalez-Haro *et al.* 2007). Those studies have demonstrated a range of BLC between 1 and up to 2.2 mmol.l^{-1} corresponding to exercise intensities from 30 to 75 % $\dot{V}O_{2peak}$ (Table 3.1). Our data support large BLC range at Fatmax (1- 2.2 mmol.l^{-1}). The high kel variability ranging from 0.54 - 4.4 (mmol.l^{-1})^2 may reflect the high variance in Fatmax, corresponding BLC, and exercise intensity as indicated by figure 3.19b.

study	Fatmax	Intensity (% $\dot{V}O_{2peak}$)	BLC mmol.l^{-1}	Protocol & subjects
Achten and Jeukendrup 2004	0.48 g.min^{-1}	61%	1.1	3-min moderately trained
This study	0.52 g.min^{-1}	47%	1.4	2-min incremental, active
Bircher *et al.* 2005	0.56 g.min^{-1}	1.32 W.kg^{-1} = 47%	1.2	3-min incremental, moderately trained
	0.49 g.min^{-1}	2.2 W.kg^{-1} = 64%	2.2	5-min incremental protocol
Bergman and Brooks 1999	0.4 kcal.min^{-1} = (trained) (0.2 untrained)	40%	2	1.5 hrs
Knechtle *et al.* 2004	114 cal.min.kg^{-1}	75%	2	3-mins incremental Endurance males
Venables *et al.* 2005	0.46 g.min^{-1}	46%	Not reported	3-min incremental Healthy

Table 3.1. Exercise intensity related to $\dot{V}O_{2peak}$ and BLC at Fatmax.

At a given BLC and $\dot{V}O_2$, an increase in kel decreases the RPY and increases fat oxidation at the same intensities (Figure 3.19a). Low kel indicates a rapid occurrence of Fatmax, whereas higher kel shifts Fatmax to a higher exercise intensity (Figure 3.19a).

The shift of the occurrence of Fatmax implies individual's ability to reserve CHO which is known to delay fatigue mechanisms, and other glycogen depletion related consequences (Ball *et al.* 1995; Below *et al.* 1995; Hargreaves 2004; Bergstrom *et al.* 1967).

The present study also shows that kel is independent of power outputs, and exercise intensity at BLC of 2 and 4 mmol.l^{-1} (Figure 3.10a, b). Therefore, predicting any exercise intensity based on a fixed level of BLC such as 1 (Achten and Jeukendrup 2004), 2 mmol.l^{-1} (Bircher *et al.* 2005), or any other fixed BLC value may not be a useful indicator for Fatmax. Power output, or exercise intensity at a given BLC (threshold or not) may be sufficient in determining fitness level, but it is inadequate for the estimation of the rates of CHO and fat combustion.

Fatmax correlated significantly with kel, and kel correlated with the intensity at Fatmax (Figures 3.16, 3.17). However, there was no correlation between Fatmax and the intensity at Fatmax (Figure 3.18), which has not been previously addressed. Recent studies reported exercise induced differences in Fatmax intensity but not in Fatmax (Gonzalez-Haro *et al.* 2007). The latter group reported significant differences between cyclists, triathletes, and mountain bikers for the intensities relative to $\dot{V}O_{2peak}$ at Fatmax but not for absolute Fatmax in g.min^{-1}. In contrast, Stephens *et al.* (2006) reported lower absolute Fat, and higher CHO oxidation for mid- than at late puberty at intensities of 40-70% $\dot{V}O_{2peak}$, which are similar to Fatmax intensities of the present experiment. This suggests that both of the latter studies (Gonzalez-Haro *et al.* 2007, Stephens *et al.* 2006) support that Fatmax and the intensity at Fatmax are independent. Therefore, exercise intensity alone may not be sufficient to describe changes in maximal fat oxidation. Based on the findings of this study it is suggested that fat oxidation descriptions may be strengthened by adding additional parameters such as kel, which may explain the variations in Fatmax and the intensity at Fatmax.

3.4.3. Comparison between exercise intensities at Fatmax and the cross-point

The results of this study show that the intensity at the cross-over point was not different from that of Fatmax which agrees with previously reported data (Venables *et al.* 2005). However, the almost identical intensities, of 40 ± 9.7% at Fatmax and 38.6 ± 9.5% of peak power at the cross-point, elicited significantly higher (p < 0.01) EE for fat and lower EE for CHO at Fatmax than those at the cross-point (4.81± 1.1 vs. 4.2 ± 1.1 kcal.min^{-1})

respectively. This indicates that the small differences in intensity at Fatmax and the cross-point reflect high differences in the utilisation of CHO and fat. This can be explained by the high steepness of the sigmoid curve at BLC levels corresponding to these intensities (Figure 3.6, 3.7). It is suggested that the difference in EE (and individually also in intensity) between Fatmax and the cross-point varies according to the individual activation of CHO combustion related to pyruvate availability as indicated by the individuals values of kel. For example, as demonstrated (Figure 3.19a, b), a subject with a low kel of 0.8 $(mmol.l-1)^2$ is likely to have the cross-point (if existed) at a very low intensity, which is lower than the intensity at Fatmax. Contrastingly, for a kel of 1.2 $(mmol.l-1)^2$, Fatmax and the cross-point occur at similar intensities. A high kel of 4 $(mmol.l-1)^2$ gives a lower exercise intensity at Fatmax than that at the cross-point.

Given that neither exercise intensity nor BLC alone are useful to predict individual cross-point, or Fatmax conditions, kel seems to serve as an indicator of differences of the intensities of the cross-point and Fatmax (Fig. 3.19a, b). These differences are reflected by that the cross-point being a function of RQ and relative EE of substrate utilisation; whereas, Fatmax is the result of relative substrate utilisation and the metabolic rate.

3.4.4. kel is independent of peak performance:

The present study illustrated that peak power, and $\dot{V}O_{2peak}$ was not correlated with kel (Figure 3.9a, b). This can be explained by CHO dominance at peak levels, which elicits similar RPY (100% RPY) in spite of high variance of the lactate levels. This will also explain the independence between peak BLC levels and kel (Figure 3.9c).

Peak values corresponded to an RQ > 1, where indirect calorimetry estimates 100% CHO combustion. High BLC like peak BLC, (and possibly near peak levels) elicit high $[H^+]$ which is buffered by $[HCO_3^-]$ causing: excess non-oxidative CO_2; and elevated $\dot{V}CO_2$; and possibly overestimated CHO, and underestimated fat oxidation (Jeukendrup and Wallis 2005). As we have shown above kel is more related to a range of submaximal intensities where fat and CHO combustion changes with any variation in exercise intensity.

3.4.5. Similarities between the BLC-RPY interrelationship and the intensity at MLSS:

Maximal lactate steady state (MLSS) is defined as the highest blood lactate concentration that can be maintained over time without continual blood lactate accumulation (Beneke and vonDuvillard 1996). Billat (2004) suggested that at MLSS-intensity RPY is approximately 90%, and the RQ around 0.95 - 1.0. MLSS varies between individuals from 2-8 mmol.l^{-1} (Billat *et al.* 2003; Beneke *et al.* 2000), and reflects exercise intensities of approximately 55-85% $\dot{V}O_{2peak}$ (Beneke 2000, Denadai *et al.* 2006, Billat *et al.* 2004).

Knowing that the present data showed a high inter-individual variability of kel between (0.5 - 4.4 mmol.l^{-1})^2, we correlated kel with exercise intensities at 90% of RPY, and found a significant positive correlation (Figure. 3.12). This level corresponded to a range of BLC of 3.8 ± 1.2 (2.1 - 6.6 mmol.l^{-1}) and intensities of 78 ± 13 (48 / 97) % relative to peak power equivalent to 82 ± 13 (54 / 107) % $\dot{V}O_{2peak}$, and RQ of 0.97. These values are close to those reported at MLSS in constant load exercise (Billat *et al.* 2004, Billat 2003). Therefore, kel may help to identify individual performance at MLSS intensity, and possibly MLSS based on incremental load tests.

MLSS, and MLSS-intensity have been shown to be independent of peak performance (Beneke *et al.* 2000). Similarly, our data showed no correlation between BLC and intensity at 90% of RPY with peak power and $\dot{V}O_{2peak}$ (Figure 3.13a, b, c, d).

Contrastingly, BLC-levels at 90% of RPY were also positively correlated with those intensities (r = 0.724, p < 0.01) (Figure 3.15), which is similar to what was recently reported about MLSS intensity (Denadai *et al.* 2006). This was coupled with a positive correlation between peak power and workload at 90% of RPY (Figure 3.14), which is similar to what was reported about MLSS workload (Beneke *et al.* 2000). This suggests that kel is a good reflector of the individual BLC changes that occur at MLSS-intensity, and therefore, kel may be a good indicator of MLSS intensity, which is in line with what (Denadai *et al.* 2006) reported, but not with (Beneke *et al.* 2000).

Training at MLSS-intensity (velocity) has been shown to improve performance indicators of $\dot{V}O_{2peak}$, velocity at $\dot{V}O_{2peak}$, time to exhaustion, and MLSS-velocity (Billat *et al.* 2004). This was coupled with no change in MLSS, which was approximately 4 mmol.l^{-1}. This level is similar to that predicted in the present results, and indicated by kel. This suggests that this highly effective training did not change kel. However, the training effects were because high metabolic rate at MLSS with unchanged RPY, resulting in an increase in CHO and therefore higher reliance on glycogen activity. This has no disadvantage if the performance time is relatively short. However, in long and ultra distance events, glycogen availability is a performance limiting factor.

There is no experimental evidence that kel can be changed by training. However, a potentially favourable effect for long distance performance would be a more economical use of CHO at given intensities, equivalent to an increase in kel. This would possibly increase MLSS, as shown via a simulation approach (Beneke 2003a), and illustrated in figure 3.20.

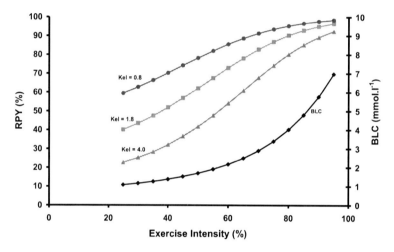

Figure 3.20 Effects of kel changes on RPY at a given BLC

It is accepted that the dominant fuel at MLSS is CHO (Billat 2003, 2004), where exercise intensities are above the cross-point. These intensities have a range of RQ around 1.0 (Billat 2003, Billat *et al.* 2004, Beneke 2000). In the data from this study, RQ at 90% of RPY is 0.97. A marathon runner runs at slightly a lower intensity than MLSS velocity (Billat *et al.* 2003). High kel for these athletes would indicate running at a lower BLC which reflects a more economical use of CHO. However, further research in trained population may be required to confirm this.

3.4.6. Limitations:

kel is a key parameter at submaximal levels but may not be meaningful at peak levels. The current data suggest that BLC availability and kel can serve as an indicator of the interaction between relative fat and CHO oxidation, but it is valid only when $RQ \leq 1$. Above this level, indirect calorimetry estimations become invalid. When RPY reaches near 100%

an excess non-oxidative CO_2, and elevates $\dot{V}CO_2$, which possibly overestimates CHO, and underestimates fat oxidation. Any increase in BLC levels at that level is assumed to reflect a saturation level of 100% RPY.

3.5. CONCLUSION:

BLC increase explains the relative increase in CHO combustion, and the interrelationship between BLC and RPY is well described sigmoidally. The steepness of the latter sigmoid interrelationship, as indicated by kel, is a good indicator for known metabolic concepts such as the cross-point, and Fatmax. Individual kel explains inter-individual variability in fat and CHO utilisation. Individual kel values seem to be a useful indicator for differences between exercise intensities corresponding to Fatmax and the cross-point. However, the variations of kel suggest that a given exercise intensity or a given BLC-level may not be meaningful to indicate substrate utilisation.

The BLC-RPY interrelationship is in agreement with MLSS concept. Individual kel may be a useful indicator for MLSS and MLSS-intensity, and may be a possible predictor of training status, though further research is required.

CHAPTER FOUR

EFFECTS OF AVERAGING $\dot{V}O_2$ AND $\dot{V}CO_2$ DATA ON THE BLC-RPY INTERRELATIONSHIP

4.1. INTRODUCTION:

From the previous chapter we concluded that the interrelationship between BLC-RPY can be described as a sigmoid function with a kel of approximately 1.8 $(mmol.l^{-1})^2$.

Depending on testing equipment and exercise protocol, $\dot{V}O_2$ and $\dot{V}CO_2$ are often sampled differently. Several averaging durations that varied between 15- up to 120s have been used during incremental testing (McDaniel et al. 2002; Woolford et al. 1999; McDaniel et al. 2005). Furthermore, the timing from the start of the stage varied from 40- up to 180s as shown in table 4.1. However, no study had investigated possible effects of differences in these averaging procedures on respiratory or metabolic indices.

Averaging the last 120s was used by Achten and Jeukendrup (2003), whereas, the last 90s was used by Nordby et al. (2006). Averaging the last 60s of $\dot{V}O_2$ and $\dot{V}CO_2$ data has also been reported for both submaximal and maximal exercise (Bourgois and Vrijens 1998; Woolford et al. 1999; Achten and Jeukendrup 2004). In contrast, the last 30-s averaging is also popular in both incremental and constant load exercise (Jones et al. 2003; Myers et al. 1990; Maeder et al. 2005). Therefore, there seems to be high variation in the best averaging and sampling procedure for respiratory data (Table 4.1).

Study	Averaging intervals of a (last segment) stage	Time from start of a stage	Protocol increment size, workload
Rossiter et al. 2006	Last 20-s	40s	1-min, 20-W
Achten et al. 2002	Last 2min (CHO/fat) Last 30-s for $\dot{V}O_{2peak}$	60-s	3-min, 35-W
Bircher et al. 2005	Last 2-min	60-s	3-min, 35-W
		120-s	5-min, 20-W
Nordby et al. 2006	Last 90-s	90s	3-min, 35-W

Sargent *et al.* 2002	Last 30-s	90s	2-min 25-W
Stephens *et al.* 2006	Every 30-s	90-s	2-min, individualised/kg
Gonzalez-Haro *et al.* 2007	Last 2-min (CHO/fat) Last 30-s for $\dot{V}O_{2peak}$	120s	4-min, 30-W
Bergman *et al.* 1999	Last 30-s	150s	3-min
Kang *et al.* 2004	Last 20-	100s	2-min 30-W
Beneke, 2003	Last 30-s	150s	3-min.
McDaniel *et al.* 2005	Last 2-min	180s	5-min

Table 4.1. Summary of different averaging protocols with different sampling durations from the start of the stage, and different intervals.

The onset kinetics of $\dot{V}O_2$, and $\dot{V}CO_2$ depends on exercise intensity (Ozyener *et al.* 2001). Different sequential components of the $\dot{V}O_2$ response within a given intensity domain can be identified. It has been established that the $\dot{V}O_2$ response is characterized by three temporal components: a) the early, usually rapid, response; b) the slower, exponential increase; and c) the steady state (Ozyener *et al.* 2001; Whipp 1994). During incremental exercise testing different averaging or sampling timing, from the start of an increment stage, may not represent the $\dot{V}O_2$ uptake accurately (Figure 4.1). Averaging or sampling an earlier segment of a stage could affect all measured values i.e. $\dot{V}O_2$, as the time to allow adaptation to corresponding steady state of $\dot{V}O_2$ shortens (Figure 4.1).

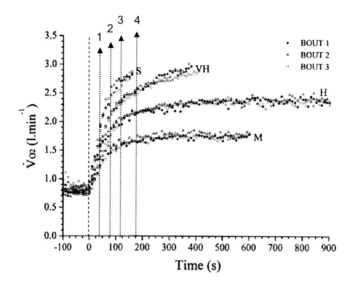

Figure 4.1. The onset kinetics of $\dot{V}O_2$ during response profiles to severe (S), very heavy (VH), heavy (H) and moderate (M) square-wave exercise for a representative subject. The three repetitions at each intensity are displayed (adapted from Ozyener *et al.* 2001). The numbers refer to varied averaging duration from the start of exercise 1. After 40-s (Rossiter *et al.* 2006) 2. After 90s (Nordby *et al.* 2006) 3.after 120s (Gonzalez-Haro *et al.* 2007) 4.after 180-s (McDaniel *et al.* 2002)

Furthermore, the onset kinetics of $\dot{V}CO_2$ is also affected by exercise intensity but differs from $\dot{V}O_2$ kinetics (Bell *et al.* 1999; Whipp 2006). The delay time as well as the time constant have been reported to be higher for $\dot{V}CO_2$ compared with $\dot{V}O_2$ at both moderate and heavy exercise intensities (Bell *et al.* 1999). Further details about the mechanisms of exchange dynamics of $\dot{V}CO_2$ and $\dot{V}O_2$ during exercise have recently been recently discussed in Whipp (2006).

Increasing the sampling or averaging interval of $\dot{V}O_2$ is likely to underestimate $\dot{V}O_2$ as shown by Myers *et al.* (1990) but there seems to be a lack of information about the effects on $\dot{V}CO_2$. To date, no study has looked at the effects of timing of averaging on both respiratory $\dot{V}O_2$ and $\dot{V}CO_2$, and indirect calorimetry. Different effects on $\dot{V}CO_2$ compared to those on $\dot{V}O_2$ are expected to influence RQ and subsequently RPY.

Previous theoretical models on the interrelationship between BLC, and RPY did not consider averaging effects because of the lack of experimental testing (Mader and Heck

1986c). Reported estimations of kel were based on 30-s averaging of the respiratory data (Beneke 2003b; Beneke 2003a). No study has evaluated the effect of averaging procedure on the BLC-RPY interrelationship.

The hypothesis of the present study is that based on a delayed response of $\dot{V}CO_2$ compared with that of $\dot{V}O_2$, the RPY decreases if the averaging period is extended to include an earlier phase of a stage, or a whole stage. Therefore, this study aimed to test whether, and how sampling of respiratory data over the last 30, 60s, or the whole stage affects the BLC-PYR interrelationship. Additionally, the effects of averaging on CHO/fat utilisation, the cross-point, and Fatmax will be investigated.

4.2. METHODS:

4.2.1. Protocol: This study is based on the same experimental protocol described in the previous chapter (Chapter 3).

4.2.2. Data Analyses: The relative exercise intensity was calculated as a percentage of peak power. Peak and submaximal $\dot{V}O_2$ and $\dot{V}CO_2$ data were averaged for the last 120, 60, and 30-s of every stage of the incremental exercise test. Pyruvate combustion and the relative rates of CHO (RPY) and fat combustion (RFAT) were estimated as previously described (Chapter 3) using the three averaging procedures of 120, 60, and 30s. Using the latter averaging procedures, RPY was further approximated as a sigmoid function of lactate (see methods of chapter 1, and 3 for details). Absolute pyruvate and fat combustion rates were calculated based on the O_2 required to oxidise glycogen, and fat (Chapter 3). Furthermore, maximal fat oxidation (Fatmax) rates and the intensities at Fatmax were determined for each individual.

To construct an average curve for the entire group, the power output, intensity, $\dot{V}O_2$, $\dot{V}CO_2$, BLC, and CHO oxidation were averaged for each incremental stage completed by all subjects. The increase in $\dot{V}O_2$, $\dot{V}CO_2$, BLC, and CHO oxidation was plotted as a function of power output.

The kel was compared for the three averaging procedures. As BLC data were unchanged by changing the averaging methods, only the differences in $\dot{V}O_2$, $\dot{V}CO_2$ were tested for differences at peak and submaximal levels. Furthermore, the averaging dependent differences for $\dot{V}O_2$ were compared to those of $\dot{V}CO_2$.

Because of the variability in exercise intensity for each subject, and to describe data for both maximal and submaximal intensities, the data was fitted using linear and nonlinear regression models for all averaging procedures (as described in chapter3). All data were described as mean ± standard deviation. Differences in averaging were compared using one way repeated measures ANOVA, and Bonferroni correction tests.

4.3. RESULTS:

Peak power was 293 ± 39.3 W. Peak $\dot{V}O_2$, $\dot{V}CO_2$, RQ were higher for averaging of 30s than 60 or 120s (p < 0.01). Furthermore, the averaging of 60 was higher than 120s (p < 0.01, (Table 4.2).

Peak	120s			60s			30s		
Data	$\dot{V}O_2$	$\dot{V}CO_2$	RQ	$\dot{V}O_2$	$\dot{V}CO_2$	RQ	$\dot{V}O_2$	$\dot{V}CO_2$	RQ
	ml.min^{-1}	ml.min^{-1}		ml.min^{-1}	ml.min^{-1}		ml.min^{-1}	ml.min^{-1}	
Mean	3684*	4038*	1.1*	3790**	4231**	1.12**	3818	4298	1.13
Stdev.	553	673	0.07	558	687	0.07	554	689	0.07

Table 4.2. Peak respiratory data for different averaging periods. *Significantly lower respiratory data than 60, and 30s. **Significantly lower than 30s.

The overall mean $\dot{V}O_2$ was lower for 120s than 60, or 30s at all submaximal workloads up to a level of 271 ± 33.9 W corresponding to an intensity of 90.1 ± 7.1% (p < 0.001). However, the $\dot{V}O_2$ data was not different between 60 and 30s, at stages below 248 ± 33.7 W (Figure 4.2).

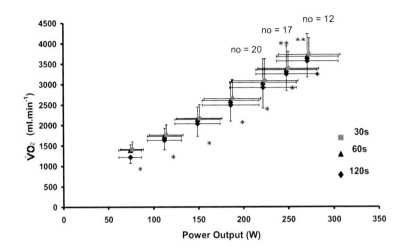

Figure 4.2. Averaging effects on submaximal $\dot{V}O_2$. *Significantly lower for 120 than 60 and 30s. **Significantly lower in 60 than 30s.

$\dot{V}CO_2$ was significantly lower for 120 than 60, or 30s at all submaximal workloads, up to a level of 186 ± 31.6 W corresponding to an intensity of 68.9 ± 10.3% of peak power (p < 0.001). $\dot{V}CO_2$ was also lower for averaging of 60- than 30s at all workloads except for stage 3 (p < 0.01), (Figure 4.3).

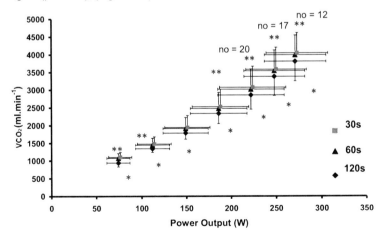

Figure 4.3. Averaging effects on submaximal $\dot{V}CO_2$. *Significantly lower in 120s than 60 and 30s. **Significantly lower in 60 than 30s

The difference in $\dot{V}CO_2$ averaging was higher than that of $\dot{V}O_2$ ($p < 0.01$) when the average duration decreased from 120 to 30s, and 60 to 30s at almost all stages (Table 4.3).

Stage no.	$\dot{V}O_2$ (ml.min^{-1}) Mean ± SD			$\dot{V}CO_2$ (ml.min^{-1}) Mean ± SD		
	120 to 60s	60 to 30s	120 to 30s	120 to 60s	60 to 30s	120 to 30s
1	174 ± 79	0 ± 48	171 ± 95	134 ± 54	27 ± 43	161 ± 75
2	101 ± 43*	10 ± 47*	111 ± 72*	104 ± 41	33 ± 50	137 ± 76
3	106 ± 30*	5 ± 58*	111 ± 63*	127 ± 37	29 ± 65	157 ± 75
4	112 ± 48*	26 ± 55*	138 ± 83*	141 ± 62	47 ± 59	188 ± 110
5 (n=20)	123 ± 38*	21 ± 39*	144 ± 56*	162 ± 54	56 ± 48	218 ± 81
6 (n=17)	103 ± 36*	10 ± 32*	114 ± 46*	167 ± 63	40 ± 60	206 ± 114
7 (n=12)	110 ± 50*	29 ± 32*	139 ± 63*	181 ± 71	54 ± 40	236 ± 91

Table 4.3. Differences induced by averaging on $\dot{V}O_2$ and $\dot{V}CO_2$. *Significantly lower than $\dot{V}CO_2$ difference.

BLC was unaffected by averaging as it was only measured once (Figure 3.3).

The steepness of the BLC-RPY curve was lower using 120s than 60s, and 30s, and for 60s than 30s (Figure 4.4).

kel was significantly higher for 120s than 60s ($p < 0.001$), and 30s ($p < 0.001$), (Table 4.4). Furthermore, kel for 60s was higher than 30s ($p < 0.001$). R-square was higher for 120s than 60s, and 30s ($p < 0.001$), but there was no difference between r-squares of 60 and 30s (Table 4.4). The individual values of kel are presented in appendix B (Table B1).

kel (mmol.l^{-1})^2	120s	r^2	60s	r^2	30s	r^2
Mean	2.566*	0.892*	2.220**	0.859	1.815	0.855
Stdev.	1.433	0.074	1.234	0.087	0.952	0.089

Table 4.4. kel values for averaging periods of 120, 60, and 30s. *Significantly higher than 60, and 30s. **Significantly higher than 30s.

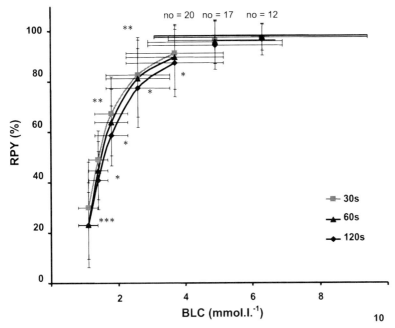

Figure 4.4. Averaging effects on BLC-RPY. *Significantly lower for 120s than 60 and 30s. **Significantly lower in 60s than 30s.***Significantly lower in 120s, and in 60 than 30s.

All individual $\dot{V}O_2$ responses were well described as a linear function of exercise intensity related to peak power for all three averaging procedures of 120, 60 and 30s respectively ($r^2 = 0.999 \pm 0.003$, 0.995 ± 0.007, 0.992 ± 0.008, all $p < 0.001$). $\dot{V}CO_2$, and BLC responses were well described as mono-exponential functions of exercise intensity ($r^2 = 0.998 \pm 0.001$, 0.998 ± 0.002, 0.997 ± 0.003 all $p < 0.001$), and ($r^2 = 0.997 \pm 0.005$, all $p < 0.001$) respectively.

The parameters describing $\dot{V}O_2$ fitting (Table B11, Appendix B) showed were significantly lower for 120s than 60 and 30s ($p < 0.001$), and not different between 60 and 30s. The parameter b was higher for 120s than 60s ($p < 0.02$), but not different between 120 and 60 or 30s.

Consequently, $\dot{V}O_2$ was lower for 120s than 60, and 30s ($p < 0.001$) at all submaximal levels. Furthermore, 60s averaging was lower than 30s at all intensities above 60% ($p < 0.01$), (Table B2, Appendix B) (Figure 4.5).

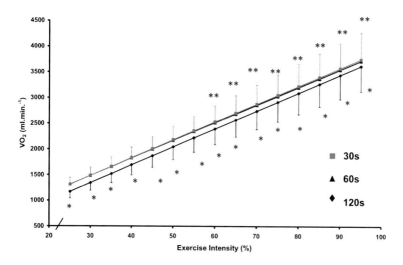

Figure 4.5. Averaging effects on $\dot{V}O_2$ at given exercise intensities. *Significantly lower $\dot{V}O_2$ in 120s than 60 and 30s. **Significantly lower $\dot{V}O_2$ in 60s than 30s.

The three parameters describing the fitting of $\dot{V}CO_2$ (a, b, and c) were not significantly different (Table B12, Appendix B).

However, $\dot{V}CO_2$ was lower for 120s than 60, and 30s ($p < 0.001$) at all submaximal intensities. Averaging 60s was also lower than 30s at all submaximal above 35% ($p < 0.001$), (Table B3, Appendix B), (Figure 4.6).

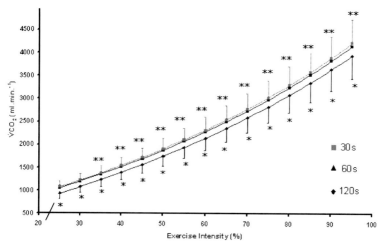

Figure 4.6. Averaging effects on $\dot{V}CO_2$ at given exercise intensities. *Significantly lower in 120 than 30, and 60s. **Significantly lower in 60 than 30s.

Furthermore, RQ was lower for 120s than 60, and 30s (p < 0.001), RQ was also lower for 60 than 30s (p < 0.01), (Table B4, Appendix B).

RPY was lower for 120s than 60 and 30s (p < 0.001), and lower for 60s than 30s (p < 0.001) at all submaximal levels up to 80% (Figure 4.7), and (Table B5, Appendix B). Consequently, RFAT was higher for 120 than 60 and 30s (p < 0.001), and higher for 60 than 30s (p < 0.001) for all submaximal levels up to 80% (Figure 4.7) and (Table B6, Appendix B).

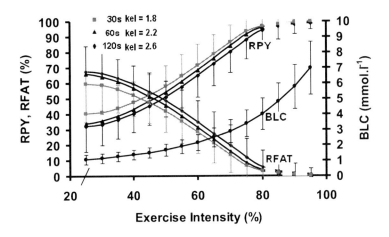

Figure 4.7. Averaging effects on the relative rates of pyruvate and fat utilisation. Significance levels are displayed in appendix B (Tables B5, B6). Increased averaging duration reduced RPY and increased RFAT.

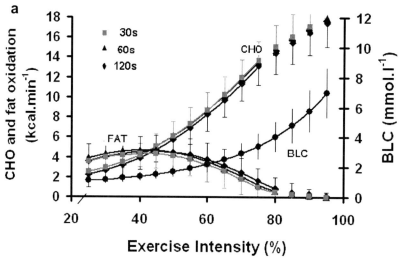

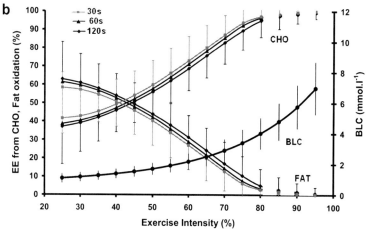

Figure 4.8 (a,b). Averaging effects on the energy expenditure of fat and CHO oxidation. Significance levels are displayed in appendix B (Table B9, B10).

The cross-point where EE from CHO becomes the predominant fuel source over fat was undetectable in 5 of the 21 subjects, due to selecting exercise intensities starting from 25%. In the remaining 16 subjects, the intensity at the cross-point was increased as averaging period increased from 30s to 60s, and 120s, and from 60s to 120s (p < 0.001), (Table 4.5). The cross point occurred at a higher BLC when averaging period was extended from 30 to 60s (p < 0.001), 60 to 120s (p=0.001), and 30 to 120s (p < 0.001).

The corresponding EE was higher for 120 and 60s than 30s (p < 0.001), but not 120 than 60s (Table 4.5), (Figure 4.8).

	The cross-point data Mean ± SD			Fatmax data Mean ± SD		
	120s	60s	30s	120s	60s	30s
Intensity (% peak power)	46.2 ± 11.0*	43.0 ± 11.4**	37.3 ± 12.6	42.6 ± 8.5	40.1 ± 9.0	40.1 ± 9.3
Intensity (% $\dot{V}O_{2peak}$)	51.9 ± 11.5*	50.9 ± 11.9**	45.7 ± 13.0	48.6 ± 10.2	49.3 ± 0.6	43.6 ± 8.9
EE (kcal.min^{-1})	4.5 ± 1.2**	4.6 ± 1.2**	4.1 ± 1.3	5.0 ± 1.2#	5.3 ± 1.2**#	4.9 ± 1.1#
BLC (mmol.l^{-1})	1.6 ± 0.5*	1.5 ± 0.5**	1.3 ± 0.4	1.5 ± 0.4	1.4 ± 0.5	1.4 ± 0.5

Table 4.5. Averaging effects on the cross-point, and Fatmax. *Significantly higher for 120s than 60 and 30s. **Significantly higher than 30s. #Significantly higher EE of Fatmax than that of the cross-point.

Absolute CHO oxidation rates were lower using 120s than 60s and 30s for all intensity levels (p < 0.05), (Table B7, B8, Appendix B). CHO oxidation was lower for 60s than 30s at intensities above 60% (p < 0.05). On the other hand, fat oxidation rate was not different between 120 and 60s at all intensity levels. However, it was higher at 120 and 60 than 30s. Figure 4.9 below illustrates the effects of averaging on absolute CHO and fat oxidation rates.

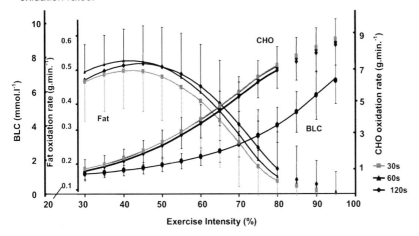

Figure 4.9. Averaging effects on the absolute rates of fat and CHO oxidation. Significance levels are displayed in appendix 2 (Table B7, B8).

Consequently, Fatmax was higher for 60s than 30s ($p < 0.001$), but was not different between 60 and 120s, or 30 and 120s. Fatmax was (0.53 ± 0.13, 0.54 ± 0.14, 0.51 ± 0.13 g.min^{-1}) for 120, 60, and 30s respectively. There was no averaging effect on the intensity or BLC at Fatmax (Table 4.5). There was no significant difference between the exercise intensities, or BLC levels at Fatmax and the cross-over point for all averaging procedures (Table 4.5). However, EE was significantly higher at Fatmax than that of the cross-point in all averaging procedures of 120, 60, and 30-s ($p < 0.001$ for all averages), (Table 4.5).

4.4. DISCUSSION:

The present study shows that extending the sampling duration of $\dot{V}O_2$ and $\dot{V}CO_2$, from 30 to 60s or to a whole incremental stage, reduces RPY leading to increases in kel from 1.82 to 2.2, and 2.6 (mmol.l^{-1})^2 ($p < 0.05$). The increase in individual levels of kel (Table B1, Appendix B) reflects a decrease in RPY at a given BLC. The present data also shows that extending the averaging period induces differential decreases in $\dot{V}O_2$ and in $\dot{V}CO_2$ respectively resulting in a lower RQ, and reduced RPY. This caused underestimation of the relative and absolute rates of CHO and overestimation of fat utilisation. Consequently, the reduction in RPY alone, or a combination of RPY and the metabolic rate affected estimations of known concepts such as the cross-over concept (Brooks and Mercier 1994), and Fatmax (Achten and Jeukendrup 2003).

It is known that it takes approximately 30s to attain 63%, 60s to attain 86% and 120s to attain 98% of the steady state amplitude of $\dot{V}O_2$ (Jones and Poole 2005). On the other hand, $\dot{V}CO_2$ is considered to reach a steady state after approximately 3-min depending on exercise intensity (Stringer *et al.* 1995).

Timing of averaging from the start of an increment stage varied among researchers according to their protocols (Table 4.1). Depending on testing protocol and equipments, averaging a shorter final fraction of a stage will naturally elicit higher $\dot{V}O_2$ and $\dot{V}CO_2$ as indicated elsewhere (Myers *et al.* 1990). Peak $\dot{V}O_2$ and $\dot{V}CO_2$ has been reported to increase up to 20% when using the last 30s compared to a whole stage of 60s in a ramp protocol (Matthews *et al.* 1987). This high difference is expected, because $\dot{V}O_2$ steady state attainment response will reflect the period between 63 and 86% of full adaptation when considering the last 30s. However, the $\dot{V}O_2$ calculated reflects 0 to 86% of the corresponding adaptation if a whole stage of 1 min is averaged. In the present finding, at peak level, the corresponding increase was approximately 3% for $\dot{V}O_2$, and 5% for $\dot{V}CO_2$ when comparing a whole stage of 120s with the last half of that stage. This difference was increased to 4%, and 7% for $\dot{V}O_2$, and $\dot{V}CO_2$ respectively when we compared averages of the whole stage with the last 30s of that stage. However, these results are affected by incomplete stages at peak level, which is not the case at submaximal level.

The difference at submaximal intensities was up to approximately, 12% in the low, 10% in the moderate, and 5% in the heavy intensity domain for $\dot{V}O_2$, when averaging a whole stage compared with the last 60s (Table B13, Appendix B). This difference reflects 0-98% versus 86-98% of $\dot{V}O_2$ steady state adaptation. A smaller $\dot{V}O_2$ difference of approximately 1% between 60, and 30s reflects 86-98%, and 95-98% of $\dot{V}O_2$ steady state adaptation. The latter difference occurred especially at intensities above 55% (Figure 4.5), which may be explained by a contribution of a $\dot{V}O_2$ slow component known to occur at heavy exercise intensity domain (Jones and Poole 2005). However, the current protocol is unable to detect the slow components, which require longer durations of more than 2-3 min in the heavy exercise domain (Pringle *et al.* 2003).

The present finding demonstrates that average period increase from 30 to 60 and 120s reduces $\dot{V}CO_2$ (Figure 4.6). The reduction was approximately 12-16% at low exercise intensity and 7-8% at high intensities (Figure 4.6), (Table B13, Appendix B). The effects induced by averaging on $\dot{V}O_2$ and $\dot{V}CO_2$ were different, which has not been tested before at all submaximal intensities. The difference was more profound in $\dot{V}CO_2$ eliciting approximately 8% higher difference in $\dot{V}CO_2$ than in $\dot{V}O_2$ at almost all incremental stages, and leading to a higher RQ at 30 vs. 120s ($p < 0.01$). This finding supports different onset kinetics of $\dot{V}O_2$ and $\dot{V}CO_2$ reported elsewhere (Figure 4.10), (Bell *et al.* 1999; Brittain *et al.* 2001; Whipp 2006).

Bell *et al.* (1999) reported different time constant (τ) and total time delay for $\dot{V}CO_2$ from $\dot{V}O_2$. Whipp (2006) explained that the time constant of $\dot{V}CO_2$ is slower than that of $\dot{V}O_2$ by approximately 10s during moderate exercise intensity (Figure 4.10). At high exercise intensities, the latter mechanisms are more complicated and influenced by bicarbonate buffering of protons contributing to a further increase in $\dot{V}CO_2$ levels. It is important to note that the present study focuses on the averaging overall effects on the BLC-RPY interrelationship, which is in the range of RQ ≤ 1 and the latter effects of buffering may be of minor importance. However, based on the present data it can not be excluded that it may be an issue at exercise intensities above 80%. Therefore, testing specific physiological mechanisms influencing the onset kinetics of $\dot{V}O_2$ and $\dot{V}CO_2$, and specifically time constants and time delays require different protocols with longer durations, is beyond the scope of this study. Further details on the latter mechanisms are well explained in Whipp (2006).

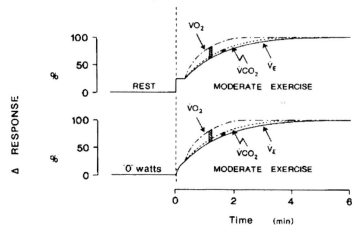

Figure 4.10. Schematic representation of time course of O_2 uptake ($\dot{V}O_2$), CO_2 output ($\dot{V}CO_2$) and ventilation ($\dot{V}_E$) in response to moderate constant-load exercise from rest. Adapted from Whipp (2006).

Therefore, different onset kinetics of $\dot{V}O_2$ and $\dot{V}CO_2$ ultimately will cause different RQ and indirect calorimetry results. For example, Bircher et al. (2005) found that averaging the last 2-mins of 5- compared with 3-min incremental protocols increases RQ from 0.79 to 0.87 at an intensity of maximal fat oxidation. This corresponded to a decrease in maximal fat oxidation of 14%, and approximately 27% increase in RPY in the 5-min stage protocols. The corresponding effects on indirect calorimetry in the present findings reflected approximately 3% increase in RFAT and reduction in RPY at almost all submaximal exercise intensities, induced by extending the averaging from the last 60s to a whole stage of 120s (Figure 4.7), (Table B5, B6, Appendix B).

The overestimation in fat and CHO at submaximal intensities reflects inappropriate estimations of many concepts that expresses performance. Those include intensities where energy from CHO predominates over fat as i.e. the cross-point (Brooks and Mercier 1994), fat oxidation is maximal i.e. Fatmax (Achten et al. 2002), and sustainability of performance with respect to glycogen stores (Beneke 2003a). At the cross-point we found significantly (p < 0.001) increased exercise intensities as the averaging duration extended (Table 4.5). This difference can be explained by a difference in the estimation of relative rates of CHO and fat utilisation. The cross-point intensities in this study (Table 4.5) were close to the 48% reported elsewhere (Venables *et al.* 2005). However, we detected an increase in the cross-point of a mean of 1% for 120s versus 60s, and 6% from 120s versus 30s (Table 4.5). In selected individuals this difference can be as high as 10% of exercise intensity which is equivalent to nearly a whole increment stage of the present protocol (Table B5, B6, Appendix B). The latter difference is equivalent to a power difference of 34 W for an average athlete weighing 75 kg. This may make the difference between winning or losing in most sports events where reserving glycogen is a limiting factor (Ball *et al.* 1995; Below *et al.* 1995).

Furthermore, the cross-point was detected at higher BLC-levels when averaging period extended (Table 4.5). Extending averaging duration induced an increase in the cross-point reflected by an increase in the level of kel (Figure 4.7). Therefore, provided that sampling and averaging procedure is carefully defined when estimating the cross point, kel is a good indicator for the cross-point. Increased kel indicates a rightward shift in the cross-point, which could mean lower dependence on CHO utilisation considered to increase exercise performance (Brooks and Mercier 1994).

Conversely, absolute fat and CHO in the present data were influenced by the averaging effects in both the RQ and metabolic rate (Figure 4.9). For CHO, the difference was approximately 1% decrease (p<0.05) for 120s versus 30s, and 60s, but became insignificant for 60s versus 30s. However, fat was increased by 1% (p<0.05) at almost all exercise intensities below 75% for 120, and 60s versus 30s, but became insignificant for 120s versus 60s (Figure 4.9) (Table B7, B8, Appendix B).Consequently, Fatmax was not different for 120s versus 60s, but significantly higher for 60s versus 30s (Figure 4.9). The overestimation of Fatmax by a mean of 0.3 g.min^{-1} equivalent to approximately 8% may affect exercise performance when it is based on estimating the ability to oxidise fat (Hollozy and Coyle 1984, in Achten *et al.* 2002).

Improving the capacity to oxidise fat has been reported to be an important factor of obesity and type-2 diabetes (Jeukendrup and Wallis 2005). Overestimated fat oxidation and EE could induce an error when training is prescribed to benefit overweight or obese individuals by improving fatty acid combustion from intramuscular triglycerides stores and adipose tissues (Brooks and Mercier 1994). However, one must note that indirect calorimetry does not distinguish between different sources of fat. Therefore, prescribing exercise intensity for optimal training of fat metabolism based on incremental exercise testing may result in too high intensities if averaging period of $\dot{V}O_2$ and/or $\dot{V}CO_2$ is too long.

We demonstrated previously that an increase in kel reflects a leftward shift in the intensity at Fatmax, and a rightward shift in the cross-point, which corresponded to a higher EE from Fatmax than the cross-point (Chapter 3). The present study demonstrated that EE from Fatmax was higher than that of the cross-point ($p < 0.01$) for all averaging periods (Table 4.5), which confirms the previous finding. Averaging increase from 30 and 60 to 120s seems to have widened the differences of the intensities at Fatmax and the cross-point, though it remained insignificant (Figure 4.7, 4.9).

Changes in the averaging duration modify the functional link between RPY and BLC and reflected by changes in kel. Therefore, kel levels seem to be influenced by the averaging effects on relative CHO and fat utilisation. Thus, applying kel for exercise testing should consider averaging duration and timing of averaging.

4.4.1. Methodological aspects:
Indirect calorimetry has widely been used for the estimation of fat and CHO utilisation (Brooks *et al.* 2005). Longer averaging duration reduces the noise to signal ratio, and has therefore proved popular among researchers (Achten *et al.* 2002, Gonzalez-Haro *et al.* 2007, Jeukendrup *et al.* 2002). The present study shows that the quality of the fit, used to estimate kel, improved with an increase in the averaging period indicated by higher r^2 for averaging 120 than 60, and 30s ($p < 0.01$) with no difference between 60 and 30s. However, based on evidence from literature regarding the onset kinetics of $\dot{V}O_2$ and $\dot{V}CO_2$ (Bell *et al.* 1999, Whipp 2006), and the present results of CHO and fat utilisation, it is recommended that the last 30s of a stage may be the best method of averaging or sampling data for the estimation of CHO and fat utilisation. Consequently, the BLC-RPY interrelationship may be more accurate if described using the latter averaging method.

It is important to note that BLC was measured only during the last 30s of each incremental stage. BLC is expected to be lower if measured earlier during an incremental stage. This may diminish the detected differences in kel because lower RPY would correspond to a lower BLC at any level. However, the consequences of different BLC cannot be confirmed until further research is conducted.

4.5. CONCLUSION:

The BLC-RPY interrelationship is affected by averaging the $\dot{V}O_2$ and $\dot{V}CO_2$ data suggesting that averaging duration and the timing of averaging should be clearly defined when applying the BLC-RPY interrelationship. Evidence from literature suggests for any test protocol that the timing should consider the onset kinetic of $\dot{V}O_2$ and $\dot{V}CO_2$. Extending the averaging period to include the whole stage induced differential decreases in $\dot{V}O_2$ and in $\dot{V}CO_2$, respectively causing underestimation of RPY and overestimation of RFAT during exercise characterised by small but significant increase in kel.

Averaging effects should be considered for exercise testing especially where the cross-point and Fatmax are used as markers to improve performance. The effects of averaging duration on absolute rates of fat and CHO estimation are different from those on the energy expenditure from CHO and fat. Consequently the cross-point and Fatmax are differently affected. The last 30-s of a 2-min stage will be used in all further chapters within this book.

CHAPTER FIVE
EFFECTS OF EXERCISE DURATION ON THE BLC-RPY INTERRELATIONSHIP

5.1. BACKGROUND AND INTRODUCTION:

It has been shown that extending the period of the averaging duration from 30s up to 120s reduced RPY at a given BLC, and increased the levels of kel, showing that kel is affected by the latter averaging effects (Chapter 4). Within chapters of this book, we used averaging of the last 30-s of each 2-min incremental stage considered to be an appropriate averaging procedure for accurately describing the BLC-RPY interrelationship (Chapter 4), and widely recommended for respiratory maximal and submaximal testing (Howley et al. 1995). However, we indicated that considering the last 30-s of longer stage duration than 2-min, may have various effects on the BLC-RPY interrelationship, which requires addressing.

In most chapters of this book a 2-min protocol was adopted as widely used in healthy and clinical settings (Sargent et al. 2002, Stephens et al. 2006; Kang et al. 2004). However, shorter, and longer incremental protocols have also been used for testing healthy adults, and elite athletes (Achten et al. 2002; Bircher et al. 2005; Beneke 2003b; Ozyener et al. 2001; Myers et al. 1990).

It is known that longer exercise durations than 2-3 minutes are preferred to achieve a steady state of $\dot{V}O_2$ and $\dot{V}CO_2$ especially at high exercise intensities (Xu and Rhodes 1999; Jones and Poole 2005; Pringle et al. 2003). It is also known that the relative rates of fat and CHO are affected by changes in exercise duration, and intensity (Ranallo and Rhodes 1998). An increase in exercise intensity increases the RPY and reduces RFAT. However, it is less clear how these rates are affected at the same intensity as duration increases. Romijn et al. (1993) demonstrated that at 65% $\dot{V}O_{2peak}$ FFA, and muscle triglycerides contribution increases on the expense of muscle glycogen and plasma glucose, and more so in a fasting state. However, similar effects at low intensities are not known, especially in incremental testing.

A 3-min protocol has been recommended for the estimation of CHO and fat utilisation, especially at maximal levels (Achten *et al.* 2002). The latter group reported no difference in fat oxidation, at its maximum or minimum levels, using 3- and 5-min incremental, or 4-6 min constant load tests. Others argue that longer durations provide different fat and CHO estimations and may be more representative to a steady state response i.e. 5, and 6-mins (Perez-Martin *et al.* 2001; Bircher *et al.* 2005).

BLC, its maximal steady state, and thresholds are known to be affected by exercise duration, and the size of the workload increment. Exercise duration of up to 10-min were recommended to achieve a steady state of BLC (Kindermann *et al.* 1979; Heck 1990; Carta *et al.* 1991; Heck and Rosskopf 1993; Stockhausen *et al.* 1994, in Stockhausen et *al.* 1997). Beneke (2003c) suggested that achieving approximately 99% of BLC steady state may require a testing duration of up to 20-min for each workload tested. However, no study related the change induced by different duration protocols on BLC, with those on the relative substrate utilisation.

Bircher *et al.* (2005) reported that longer stage duration of 5- versus 3-min of incremental protocols increased BLC, and RQ at intensities corresponding to maximal fat oxidation. They suggested that stage duration influences the BLC-threshold, and its indication of fat oxidation. However, they did not report the effects for all exercise intensity levels, and did not consider the duration effects on both BLC and RPY in a unified system.

Chapter four has shown that the BLC-RPY interrelationship is affected by different averaging or sampling protocols. It has been shown that the differential onset kinetics of $\dot{V}O_2$ and $\dot{V}CO_2$ resulted in a different RQ, and therefore, different RPY at given BLC levels (Chapter 4). However, longer stage duration may alter both BLC and RPY. Based on the shown interrelationship between BLC and RPY, a change in RPY is likely to be indicated by a change in BLC levels. Therefore, the hypothesis of the present study is that different stage durations affect BLC, and RPY, but does not change the BLC-RPY interrelationship.

5.2. METHODS:

5.2.1. Subjects and protocol:

Eleven healthy male subjects (age: 29.7 ± 5.6 years, height: 180.6 ± 5.9 cm, body mass: 74.5 ± 6.2 kg) completed two incremental load cycling tests of two, and six minutes in random order in different occasions within a period of two weeks. Both tests were performed at similar time of the day. For both protocols the power output was initiated and increased by 0.5 $W.kg^{-1}$ body mass until volitional exhaustion, and pedalling rate remained constant at 50 rpm. Capillary blood samples were drawn at rest and at the end of every 2-min for the 2-min protocol, and every 2, 4 and 6 min for the 6-min protocol. Blood samples were analysed for lactate as described previously in the general methods (Chapter 2).

5.2.2. Data analyses and statistics:

Peak power and relative exercise intensities were determined as described in chapter 3. At submaximal levels two comparisons were conducted: 1) 2-min versus 6-min protocol; and 2) segments of every 2 minutes within the 6-min protocol. All data was described as a function of workload for each of the completed stages by all subjects, and further fitted linearly and non-linearly as a function of exercise intensities as described in chapter 3. The magnitude of the BLC-RPY interrelationship was compared for 2-min versus 6-min protocol. The magnitude of the BLC-RPY was also compared for 2nd, 4th, and 6th min within the 6-min protocol, using the BLC, and RPY within each 6-min stage.

All descriptive data were presented as mean ± standard deviation. Differences were tested using repeated measures ANOVA, and Bonferroni post hoc tests. Paired t-test was also used where appropriate. Correlations were tested using Pearson's product-moment test.

5.3. RESULTS:

5.3.1. Comparison between 2- and 6-min protocols:

5.3.1.1. Peak Data:

Peak power, BLC, and $\dot{V}CO_2$ were higher for the 2- than 6-min (p < 0.01). However, there was no difference for $\dot{V}O_2$ (Table 5.1). Higher $\dot{V}CO_2$ resulted in a significantly higher (p < 0.001) RQ for 2- than 6-min (Table 5.1).

Peak data	2-min	6-min
Power (W)	302.2 ± 49.3	258.5 ± 35.3*
BLC (mmol.l^{-1})	10.4 ± 1.6	8.7 ± 2.1*
$\dot{V}O_2$ (ml.min^{-1})	3844 ± 603	3906 ± 610
$\dot{V}CO_2$ (ml.min^{-1})	4579 ± 712	4102 ± 604*
RQ	1.19 ± 0.04	1.05 ± 0.03*

Table 5.1. Peak data at 2 vs. 6 min protocols. *Significantly lower than 2 min.

5.3.1.2. Submaximal data:

Except for the initial stage $\dot{V}O_2$ and $\dot{V}CO_2$ were higher for the 6 than 2-min at all submaximal workloads below 186.8 ± 15.0 W (p < 0.01), (Figure 5.1, 5.2), corresponding to intensities of 63 ± 9.5 for 2-min and 73.2 ± 9.5 % for 6-min.

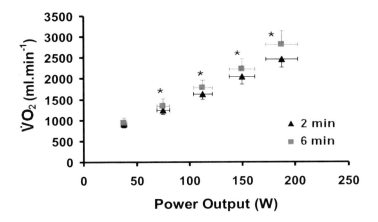

Figure 5.1. $\dot{V}O_2$ data for stages completed by all subjects in both 2- and 6-min protocols. *Significantly higher for 6-min than 2-min.

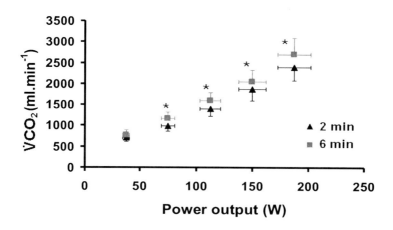

Figure 5.2. V̇CO₂ data for stages completed by all subjects in both 2- and 6-min protocols. *Significantly higher for 6-min than 2-min.

There was no difference in BLC for all workloads below 186.8 ± 15.0 W (Figure 5.3).

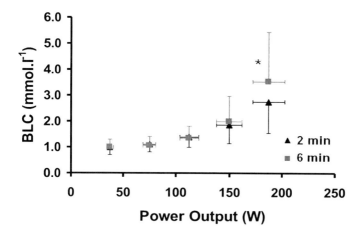

Figure 5.3. BLC data for stages completed by all subjects in both 2- and 6-min protocols. *Significantly higher for 6-min than 2-min.

There was also no difference in RPY between 2- and 6-mins for all submaximal workloads up to 186.8 ± 15.0 W (Figure 5.4).

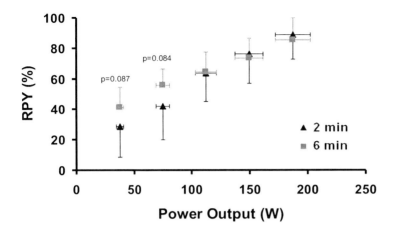

Figure 5.4. RPY data for stages completed by all subjects in both 2- and 6-min protocols.

The coefficient of determination for the fitted submaximal data of $\dot{V}O_2$, $\dot{V}CO_2$ and BLC were (0.995 ± 0.003, 0.998 ± 0.002 and 0.997 ± 0.005) for 2-min, and (0.990 ± 0.007, 0.998 ± 0.001 and 0.997 ± 0.005) for 6-min, respectively ($p < 0.001$).

Figure 5.5 illustrates that there are no differences induced by different stage durations on BLC and RPY at given submaximal exercise intensities ($p > 0.05$).

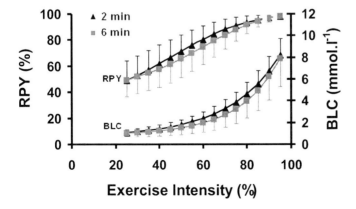

Figure 5.5. BLC and RPY responses to different durations at given exercise intensities

kel was not significantly different (1.241 ± 0.523 vs. 1.164 ± 0.788 (mmol.l^{-1})^2), (r^2 = 0.82 ± 0.13 vs. 0.84 ± 0.13) for the 2, and 6-min respectively (Figure 5.6). Individual kel data are presented in (Table C1, Appendix C).

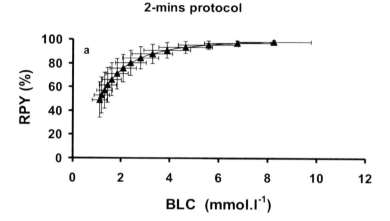

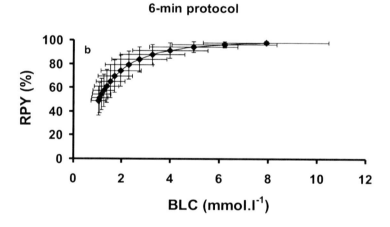

Figure 5.6. RPY as a function of BLC for 2- (a) and 6-min (b) protocols

However, there was no correlation between kel at 2-, and 6-min (Figure 5.7).

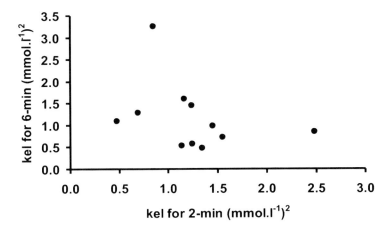

Figure 5.7. No correlation between kel at 2- and 6-min protocols

There was no difference between Fatmax (0.37 ± 0.16 vs. 0.39 ± 0.15 g.min^{-1}) for 2- and 6-min, respectively. Fatmax intensity was 6.4 % higher (41.4 ± 11.0 vs. $35.0 \pm 10.7\%$) for 6 than 2-min respectively, but not significant ($p = 0.056$). Furthermore, BLC at Fatmax was not different (1.2 ± 0.3 vs. 1.2 ± 0.3 mmol.l^{-1}) for 2- and 6-min respectively.

5.3.2. Comparisons within 6-min protocol:

Submaximal data of $\dot{V}O_2$ and $\dot{V}CO_2$ were not different between 2nd, 4th, and 6th min at workloads below 186.8 ± 15.0 W ($p < 0.01$), (Figure 5.8, 5.9) corresponding to exercise intensities of 73.2 ± 9.5 % for 6-min. However, higher workloads up to a workload of 260.4 ± 23.4 W corresponding to an intensity of $91.2 \pm 9.9\%$ elicited higher 6th min $\dot{V}O_2$ and $\dot{V}CO_2$ than 2-min ($p < 0.01$), (Figure 5.8, 5.9).

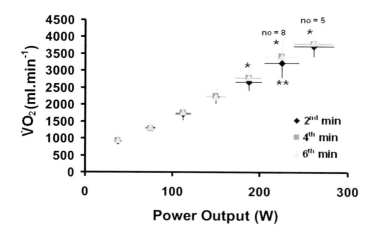

Figure 5.8. Submaximal $\dot{V}O_2$ data during the 2nd, 4th, and 6th minute of the 6-min protocol. *Significantly higher in 6th than 2nd min.**Significantly higher in 4th than 2nd min.

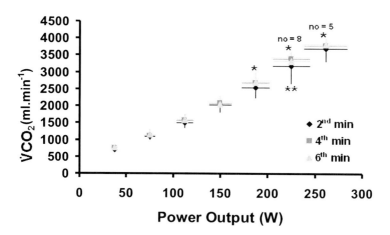

Figure 5.9. Submaximal $\dot{V}CO_2$ data during the 2nd, 4th, and 6th minute of the 6-min protocol. *Significantly higher in 6th than 2nd min.**Significantly higher in 4th than 2nd min.

BLC was unchanged between 2nd, 4th, and 6th min at workloads below 149.5 ± 12.0 W. However, BLC was higher for 6th, and 4th than 2nd min at higher workloads up to 224.3 ± 20.0 W corresponding to exercise intensities of 83.3 ± 10.1% ($p < 0.01$), (Figure 5.10).

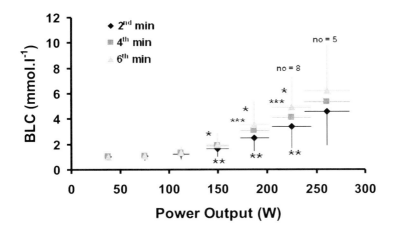

Figure 5.10. Submaximal BLC data during the 2nd, 4th, and 6th minute of the 6-min protocol. *Significantly higher in 6th than 2nd min.**Significantly higher in 4th than 2nd min. ***Significantly higher in 6th than 4th min.

Except for stage 1 and 2 RPY was not different between 2nd, 4th, and 6th min of exercise at all submaximal workloads up to 260.4 ± 23.4 corresponding to an intensity of 91.2 ± 9.9% (Figure 5.11).

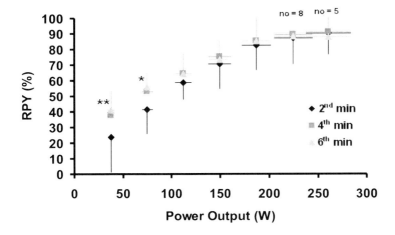

Figure 5.11. RPY data at submaximal workloads during the 2nd, 4th, and 6th minute of the 6-min protocol. *Significantly higher in 4th and 6th than 2nd min. **Significantly lower in 2nd than 6th min.

The coefficient of determination for the fitted submaximal data were (0.992 ± 0.007, and 0.998 ± 0.002) in the 2nd, (0.990 ± 0.007, and 0.998 ± 0.001) in the 4th min, and (0.990 ± 0.007, and 0.998 ± 0.002) in the 6th min for $\dot{V}O_2$, $\dot{V}CO_2$ and BLC respectively ($p < 0.001$).

Figure 5.12 illustrates the differences induced by different segments of a 6-min protocol on BLC and RPY at submaximal exercise intensities.

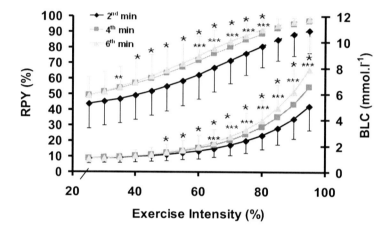

Figure 5.12. BLC and RPY data at submaximal exercise intensities for the 2nd, 4th, and 6th minute of the 6-min exercise protocol. *Significantly higher in 4th and 6th than 2nd min. **Significantly higher in 6th than 2nd min.***Significantly higher in 6th than 4th and 2nd.

kel was not significantly different (1.558 ± 1.214, 1.217 ± 0.779, 1.164 ± 0.788 $(mmol.l^{-1})^2$), (r^2 = 0.784 ± 0.166, 0.788 ± 0.101, 0.84 ± 0.13) for 2nd, 4th, and 6th min respectively (Figure 5.13). Individual kel data are presented in (Table C3, Appendix C).

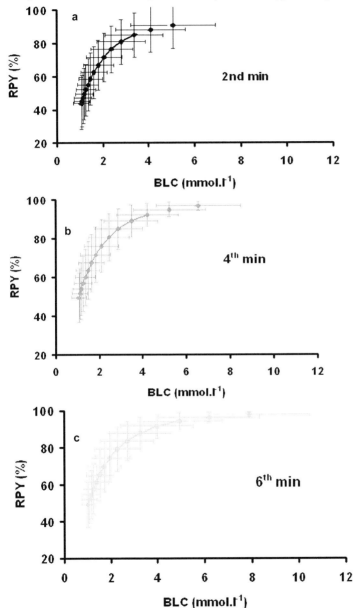

Figure 5.13. RPY as a function of BLC at the 2nd (a) 4th (b) and 6th min (c) within a 6-min incremental protocol.

Furthermore, kel at the 2nd min correlated significantly (p < 0.01) with the 4th and 6th min (Figure 5.14). kel of the 4th also correlated significantly (p< 0.01) with that of the 6th min (Figure 5.15).

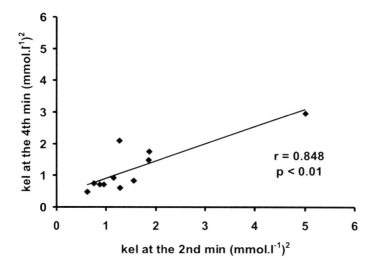

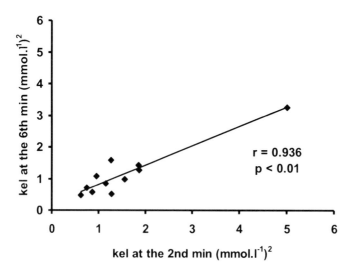

Figure 5.14. Significant correlation between kel at the 2nd with 4th and 6th min

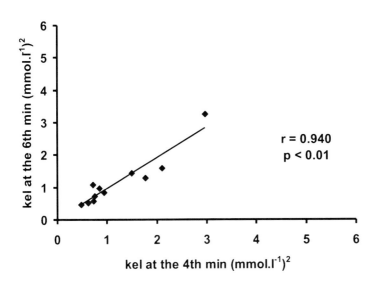

Figure 5.15. Significant correlation between kel at the 2nd with 4th and 6th min

However, the latter correlation were affected by an outlier for kel calculated in the 2nd min in subjects number 9 (kel = 5 > 3*SD), (Table C3, Appendix C). Deleting the latter case weakened the correlations between 2nd and 4th, and 2nd and 6th (r = 0.65 p = 0.044), and (r = 0.67, p = 0.034) respectively (Figure 5.16, 5.17). In the comparison between 4th and 6th min, no effects were observed upon deleting the same case (r = 0.90, p = 0.01), (Figure 5.18).

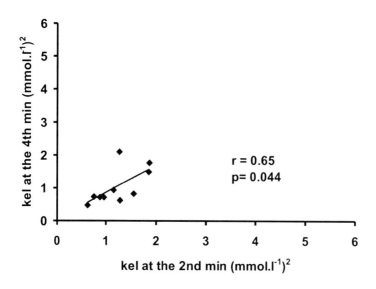

Figure 5.15. Significant correlation between kel at the 2nd with 4th min (n = 10)

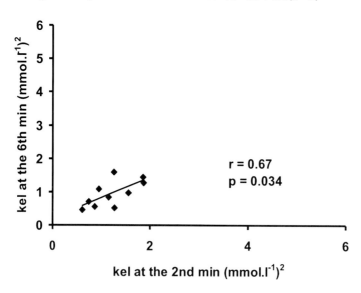

Figure 5.17. Significant correlation between kel at the 2nd with 6th min (n = 10)

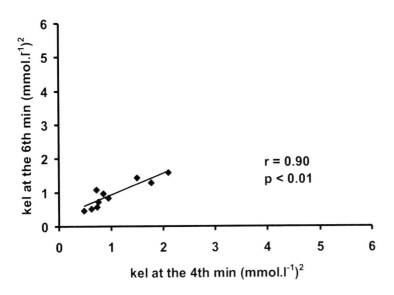

Figure 5.18. Correlation between kel at the 4th with 6th min (n = 10)

The F-values, estimated based on the degree of freedom and residual sum of squares, reflected the latter effects by a reduction in the significance level from $p<0.01$ to $p<0.05$ for 2nd vs. 4th , and 6th , but not for 4th vs. 6th ($p<0.01$). The F-values were (23.1 vs. 5.7) for 2nd vs. 4th, (63.5 vs. 6.5) for 2nd vs. 6th, and (67.8 vs. 32.3) for 4th vs. 6th.

5.4. DISCUSSION

The first main finding of the present study is that kel was not different at different stage durations whether analysing 2- and 6-min protocols, or 2nd, 4th and 6th min in a 6-min protocol. The second main finding is that kel of the 2 and 6-min protocols did not correlate whilst significant correlations were found between the 2nd and 4th, the 2nd and 6th, and the 4th and 6th min of the 6-min protocol. However, in spite of the fact that no difference in kel was determined by different stage durations, the present data do not suggest that the BLC-RPY interrelationship is independent of stage duration because of the lack of correlation between 2- and 6-min protocols (Figure 5.7). The latter seemed to be supported by the observation that the correlation between 4th and 6th was higher than that between the 2nd and 4th and 2nd and 6th min (Figure 5.14, 5.15, 5.16, 5.17, 5.18).

The present data shows that in both protocols BLC did not change at all power outputs below that of stage 4 (Figure 5.3), and also within 6-min protocol (Figure 5.10). Conversely, RPY increase was apparent when using 6- vs. 2-min only in the first two stages (Figure 5.4), though this was not significant. This difference became significant when the comparison was done within a 6-min protocol between the 2nd versus 4th and 6th min within 6-min protocol (Figure 5.11). However, at higher power outputs when BLC started to increase, and the difference in BLC response to different protocols appeared, RPY levels were not different and already reaching 80% close to the saturation level. This shows that BLC did not reflect RPY changes neither at low nor at high power outputs, which may explain the protocol related lack of correlation between 2- and 6-min protocols in spite of similar kel levels. This also explains the weaker correlation observed between 2nd and 4th, 2nd and 6th, but not between 4th and 6th min within 6-min protocol. The present data suggest that different protocols should not be compared as both BLC and RPY were affected by the protocol at different stages.

No RPY difference shown in figure 5.5, especially at the lower exercise intensities do not seem to be comparable with that of the workload difference in figure 5.4. Averaged workloads presented in figure 5.4 represents different exercise intensities i.e. 70 W may represent 23% exercise intensity for a subject, and 27% for another. Additionally, there might be further effects of high standard deviation of RPY, especially at low workloads, contributing to the non significant difference seen in figure 5.4. BLC was affected by the different protocols and did not change at lower workloads (Figure 5.3), remaining near resting values for the first three stages, and increased at the higher workloads in 6 than 2-

min (Figure 5.3). However, at given intensities BLC showed similar increase in both 2- and 6-min protocols mainly because of the BLC changes within the same workload at 6-min, which was not reflected at given exercise intensities (Figure 5.5). Therefore, fitting the data clarified RPY response at given exercise intensities (Figure 5.5). Thus, comparing these protocols based on identical relative intensities and stage duration seems to partly compensate for the obvious effects at given workloads.

The latter effects of duration on the BLC and RPY within one protocol (Figure 5.12) reflected no difference in kel, which is not a fully convincing case. A better observed coefficient of determination that is affected by stage duration (though not significant) between the 4th and 6th than 2nd min make us favour a longer exercise duration of 4, or 6-min for a better description of the BLC-RPY interrelationship. Further research with longer protocols may be required to clarify longer duration effects on kel.

The onset kinetics of $\dot{V}O_2$ reaches >99% of its steady state attainment after approximately 3 min of exercise i.e. after four time constants have elapsed, though this may take longer at higher intensities (Jones and Pool, 2005). The present finding demonstrate lower $\dot{V}O_2$ at 2- than 6-min protocol (Figure 5.1), particularly at higher workloads, and at 2nd compared with 4th and 6th min within 6-min protocol, reflecting 95-98% versus > 99% $\dot{V}O_2$ adaptation attainment. The effects of stage duration on $\dot{V}O_2$ are also expected for $\dot{V}CO_2$ (Figure 5.2, 5.9). The contribution of an additional non aerobic CO_2 in the severe intensity domain corresponding to > 80% may add an additional factor to an increased $\dot{V}CO_2$ in both 2, and 6-min protocols.

The different onset kinetics of $\dot{V}O_2$ from that of $\dot{V}CO_2$ has previously been shown to explain RPY differences induced by different averaging methods (Chapter 4). These effects are characterised by a different time constant and time delay (Bell et al. 1999, Whipp 2006). In the present finding, the latter effects may explain higher RPY for 6- than 2-min in the first two stages (Figure 5.4), and at 4th and 6th than 2nd min within 6-min protocol (Figure 5.11). This suggests that a small change in RQ for 2-min elicited significant change in RPY (Figure 5.5, 5.12). The effects of different $\dot{V}CO_2$ onset kinetics were less apparent at higher power outputs possibly due to the $\dot{V}O_2$ slow component (Pringle et al. 2003) in the sever intensity domain in the 6-min protocol, which may have reduced the latter difference (Figure 5.5, 5.12).

Reaching a steady state of BLC takes longer to stabilise than other physiological measures, and depends on exercise intensity and duration (Mader *et al.* 1976; Rusko *et al.* 1986; Heck 1990; in Stockhausen *et al.* 1997). It has been suggested in incremental exercise that a workload increment of 50 W requires at least 5-min to achieve BLC steady state, which is higher than 10 W increment size required in 2-min protocol (Stockhausen *et al.* 1997). This supports, and explain the higher BLC detected in the present study when using the same increment size of 0.5 $W.kg.min^{-1}$ equivalent to approximately 45 W in both protocols of 2- and 6-min (Figure 5.3), and at the 6th minute compared with the 2nd and 4th (Figure 5.10).

At several work rates a steady state of BLC has been reported after 10-15 min (Margaria *et al.* 1933, 1963 in Billat *et al.* 2003). Stockhausen *et al.* (1997) reported that attaining 95% of BLC steady state requires approximately 5-9 min and is influenced by the workload. Others reported that longer duration protocols of at least 20-min achieve 99% of MLSS corresponding to approximately 4.9 $mmol.l^{-1}$ (Beneke 2003c). The latter reported that lower workloads require less time to achieve MLSS, and that the increase in BLC, depending on the workload, increases the time constant, which can take up to 20-min. Figure 5.12 illustrates no adaptation in BLC up to intensity of 50%. However, as BLC levels increase, the time constant is increased at the higher intensities of approximately 65%. Further increases in BLC levels at intensities > 65% show that 4th and 6th min are possibly not long enough to reflect BLC adaptation, which supports the previous finding (Beneke 2003c). This suggestion is based on a combination of the difference between 4th and 6th min, and the literature data suggesting longer duration for BLC adaptations (Beneke 2003c, Stockhausen *et al.* 1997). However, this study did not test durations beyond 6th min, and further research may be required.

The present effects of exercise duration on the BLC-RPY interrelationship (Figures 5.6, 5.13) have not been studied before. However, similar effects on BLC, respiratory data, and indirect calorimetry have been reported when extending exercise duration from 3- to 5-min increment stages (Bircher *et al.* 2005). At exercise intensities corresponding to Fatmax, the latter reported an higher BLC of approximately 1 $mmol.l^{-1}$. This was coupled with 0.08 higher RQ which is equivalent when calculated to approximately 27% higher RPY for 5- than 3-min protocol. The corresponding effects in the present data showed no difference in BLC or Fatmax between 2- and 6-min protocols. However, Fatmax intensity was approximately 6.4% higher, though not significant ($p = 0.056$). This is expected as exercise intensities for the 6-min are based on lower peak power than those for the 2-min protocol (Table 5.1). Therefore, a reduction in stage duration from 6 to 2-min does not seem to affect Fatmax, or Fatmax intensity which is in line with Achten *et al.* (2002), but not with Bircher *et al.* (2005).

5.4.1. Limitations:

The results of this study suggest that kel values obtained from different protocols does not entirely detect the effects on the BLC-RPY. kel may be affected by the design of the protocol. The results also suggest that it is not possible to use protocols with incremental stage duration of more than 6-min for kel because of an insufficient data points to estimate kel. Future studies aiming to investigate the effects of longer exercise durations on the BLC-RPY interrelationship may require testing each exercise intensity in separate occasion.

5.5. CONCLUSION:

In spite of no change in kel, the present finding suggest that the BLC-RPY is affected by increased stage duration from 2 to 6-min. The lack of correlation between kel between 2- and 6-min protocols, and stronger correlation between 4th and 6th than that between 2nd and 4th or 2nd and 6th min within 6-min protocol, suggest an alteration of the BLC-RPY interrelationship. Perhaps kel is not enough to describe the BLC-RPY interrelationship entirely. However, increased stage duration affects BLC and RPY differently, suggesting that comparing different protocols may be irrelevant for detecting changes in kel. Based on the adaptations of BLC and the onset kinetics of $\dot{V}O_2$ and $\dot{V}CO_2$, it may be appropriate to use exercise stage duration of at least 4-min for a better description of the BLC-RPY interrelationship.

CHAPTER SIX
EFFECTS OF CYCLING CADENCE ON THE BLC-RPY
INTERRELATIONSHIP

6.1. INTRODUCTION:

Different modes of exercise have different impacts on performance and metabolic capacity. Treadmill exercise testing has been shown to elicit higher peak oxygen uptake ($\dot{V}O_{2peak}$), and a higher heart rate than bicycle ergometer, because it involves larger muscle groups (Maeder *et al.* 2005). At the same cycling ergometer exercise, different pedalling rates are the result of different muscle contraction frequency, and shortening velocity leading to various physiological acute responses. High pedalling rate increases the frequency of muscle activation and relaxation velocity compared to a lower rate leading to a higher BLC, $\dot{V}O_2$ and $\dot{V}CO_2$ at both maximal and submaximal exercise intensities.

BLC levels have been used to indicate pedalling rate effects on power output, and exercise intensity. High pedalling rate has been shown to elicit higher power output at the same BLC-threshold, defined as the second deflection point, (Woolford *et al.* 1999). In a constant load exercise test, Denadai *et al.* (2006) found that the exercise intensity, and workload at MLSS were approximately 10%, and 20% higher during cycling at 50 than 100 rpm respectively. This was coupled with no effects of MLSS which remained constant at approximately 5.0 mmol.l^{-1}. These studies suggest that BLC may be a good indicator for pedalling rate dependent effects.

 Little attention has been paid to the effects of pedalling rate on the relative utilisation of CHO and fat since the work of Gollnick *et al.* (1974). This group investigated work intensities equivalent to 30-150% $\dot{V}O_{2peak}$ with pedalling rates of 30-120 rpm, and suggested that higher cadence is associated with higher CHO utilisation due to a higher recruitment of type-II muscle fibres. A similar increase has been reported in a later study at 100 versus 50 rpm, which has not been related to muscle fibre type (Ahlquist *et al.* 1992).

It is accepted that higher pedalling rate elicit higher BLC, $\dot{V}O_2$, and $\dot{V}CO_2$ at given submaximal exercise intensities. However, it is not established whether pedalling rate increase peak power. Higher peak power, peak BLC, and $\dot{V}O_{2peak}$ have been reported when cycling at 120 compared with 40, 60, 80, and 100 rpm, without any peak power difference for between 40 and 100 rpm (Zoladz et al. 2000).At submaximal levels, power output was higher at BLC of 2, and 4 mmol.l^{-1} with no difference in $\dot{V}O_2$ as pedalling rate increased. In a later study with a similar protocol, Zoladz et al. (2002) reported higher BLC and $\dot{V}O_2$ for 120 than those for 60 rpm at all submaximal intensities below 70% $\dot{V}O_{2peak}$, without reporting the effects on peak data. Higher peak BLC but not $\dot{V}O_2$ was reported at 90 compared with 60 rpm (von Duvillard and Hagan 1994). This shows that there is no agreement in the literature about the responses of BLC, and $\dot{V}O_2$ to different pedalling rates at both peak and submaximal levels. It is not clear from the previous studies whether the latter cadence induced discrepancies can be explained by fuel mix changes. No study has linked changes in BLC levels to explain differences in the fuel mix.

Previously investigated effects of pedalling rates on substrate utilisation did not seem to link it with changes in lactate levels (Zoladz et al. 2002, Kang et al. 2004). Kang et al. (2004) found higher RQ, and total energy expenditure (EE) from CHO and fat at 80 vs. 40, or 60 rpm when cycling at 40% $\dot{V}O_{2peak}$ for 10-min. However, they found higher CHO oxidation without a difference in fat oxidation, suggesting that higher cadence induced increase in $\dot{V}O_2$ may be responsible (Kang et al. 2004). However, the latter study did not measure BLC, or linked the cadence dependent effects on CHO to changes in BLC. Hughes et al. (1982) reported higher BLC association with glycogen availability when cycling at 90 compared with 50 rpm in an incremental exercise. The latter study reported higher BLC and RQ at all submaximal workloads with no difference in $\dot{V}O_2$. To date, no study linked jointly the effects of different pedalling rates on relative use of CHO and fat utilisations, with those on BLC levels.

Chapter 3 has shown a sigmoid link between BLC levels and RPY as approximated by levels of kel. Chapter 4 and 5 have shown how the BLC-RPY interrelationship is affected by the data processing, averaging and duration protocol. Cadence has been shown to influence BLC and/or RPY (Zoladz et al. 2002; Ferguson et al. 2001). However, it is not clear whether previously seen cadence induced effects on both BLC and RPY can affect the BLC-RPY interrelationship.

Thus, this study will investigate the effects of cycling cadence on the BLC-RPY interrelationship. Different pedalling rates affect BLC, and RPY, but any change in BLC is expected to indicate a change in RPY. We hypothesize that different cadence does not affect the interrelationship between BLC and RPY, and that RPY is regulated by the availability of pyruvate indicated by BLC levels, irrespective of cycling cadence.

6.2. METHODS

Eleven healthy male subjects (age 23.5 ± 3.8 years, height, 180.3 ± 9.9 cm, body mass, 76.6 ± 14.3 kg) completed two separate incremental load cycling tests to exhaustion within a period of two weeks. Both tests were performed at similar time of the day. Pedalling rates of 50, and 100 rpm were applied on an electrically braked cycle Ergometer, (Lode Excalibur Sport, the Netherlands), in random order. Seat and handle bar height and angle were recorded for the first test and reproduced for the subsequent test. The power output was initiated to correspond to 1 $W.kg^{-1}$ body mass, and increased by 0.5 $W.kg^{-1}$ body mass, every two minutes. Subjects cycled until volitional exhaustion, which was defined as the inability to maintain the required pedalling rate for longer than 15 seconds. Capillary blood samples were drawn at rest and at the end of every 2-min stage, and further analysed as previously described (Chapter 2). $\dot{V}O_2$ and $\dot{V}CO_2$ were collected and analysed as described in the general methods (Chapter 2).

Relative exercise intensities were calculated as a percentage of peak power, and determined as explained in chapter 3. The RPY was estimated from $\dot{V}O_2$ and $\dot{V}CO_2$ using indirect calorimetry, and further described as a sigmoid function of BLC, as described in the methods section of chapter 3. $\dot{V}O_2, \dot{V}CO_2$, and BLC data were fitted using linear and nonlinear regression models as described in chapter 3.

Descriptive data were presented as mean $\pm$ SD. Differences between the two pedalling rates were tested using paired t-test and repeated measures ANOVA with Bonferroni post hoc test. Correlation coefficients were tested using Pearson's product-moment correlation coefficient.

6.3. RESULTS:

Peak power was not different for cycling at 100 compared with 50 rpm (Table 6.1). However, peak BLC was significantly higher at 100 than 50 rpm ($p < 0.01$), (Table 6.1). $\dot{V}O_{2peak}$ and $\dot{V}CO_{2peak}$ were not different (Table 6.1).

Peak data	50 RPM	100 RPM
Power (W)	295.7 ± 45.6	298.7 ± 55.8
BLC (mmol.l^{-1})	9.3 ± 1.9	11.1 ± 2.4*
$\dot{V}O_2$ (ml.min^{-1})	4045 ± 561	4131 ± 681
$\dot{V}CO_2$ (ml.min^{-1})	4638 ± 618	4712 ± 743
RQ	1.15 ± 0.08	1.14 ± 0.06

Table 6.1. Peak data for cycling at 50 and 100 rpm. *Significantly higher than 50 rpm.

$\dot{V}O_2$ was increased ($p < 0.05$) almost linearly in every stage by 385 ± 47, and 446 ± 74 ml.min^{-1} at 100 and 50 rpm respectively. The increase was not different between 100 and 50 rpm (Figure 6.1). $\dot{V}O_2$ was higher for cycling at 100 than 50 rpm at all stages corresponding to submaximal intensities between 25 ± 4 and 76 ± 11% of peak power ($p < 0.01$), (Figure 6.1).

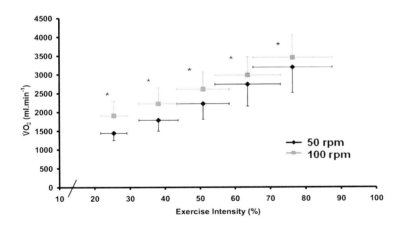

Figure 6.1. Submaximal $\dot{V}O_2$ data for stages completed by all subjects at 100 and 50 rpm. *Significantly higher than 50 rpm.

Similarly $\dot{V}CO_2$ increased ($p < 0.05$) in every stage by 479 ± 84, and 508 ± 102 ml.min^{-1} at 100 and 50 rpm respectively (Figure 6.2). The increase in $\dot{V}CO_2$ was not different between 100 and 50 rpm. $\dot{V}CO_2$ was higher at 100 than 50 rpm at all submaximal intensities between 25 ± 4 and 76 ± 11% of peak power ($p < 0.05$), (Figure 6.2).

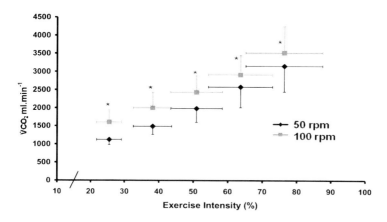

Figure 6.2. Submaximal $\dot{V}CO_2$ data for stages completed by all subjects at 100 and 50 rpm. *Significantly higher than 50 rpm.

BLC increased ($p < 0.05$) in every stage. The increase became progressively steeper above stage 4 corresponding to exercise intensities of 51 ± 7% for both 100 and 50 rpm ($p < 0.05$), (Figure 6.3). BLC was higher at 100 than 50 rpm at the all stages corresponding to submaximal intensities up to 76 ± 11% ($p < 0.05$), (Figure 6.3).

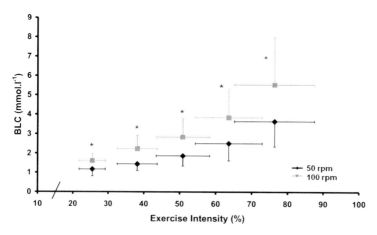

Figure 6.3. Submaximal BLC data for stages completed by all subjects at 100 and 50 rpm. *Significantly higher than 50 rpm.

RPY increased continuously in every stage (p < 0.05), but the increase started to diminish in all stages at 50 rpm, and above stage 3 corresponding to 51 ± 7% at 100 rpm (p < 0.05), (Figure 6.4).

RPY was higher at 100 than 50 rpm at all submaximal intensities below 76 ± 11% of peak power (p < 0.01), (Figure 6.4). The differences between 100 and 50 rpm diminished after the 4th stage at higher intensities (p < 0.05), (Figure 6.4).

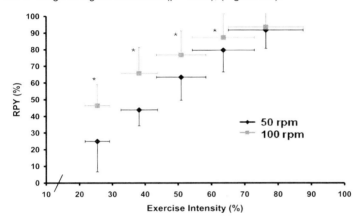

Figure 6.4. Submaximal RPY data for stages completed by all subjects at 100 and 50 rpm. *Significantly higher than 50 rpm.

The coefficient of determination for the fitted submaximal data were (0.988 ± 0.009, 0.996 ± 0.002 and 0.997 ± 0.005) at 50 rpm, and (0.983 ± 0.017, 0.995 ± 0.005 and 0.998 ± 0.004) at 100 rpm, for $\dot{V}O_2$, $\dot{V}CO_2$ and BLC respectively (p < 0.001).

The two parameters (a, b) describing $\dot{V}O_2$ fitting (Table D6, Appendix D), showed significantly lower (a) and higher (b) for 50 than 100 rpm (p < 0.001). The three parameters describing $\dot{V}CO_2$ (a, b, c) were not different between 50 and 100 rpm (Table D7, Appendix D). Figures 6.5, and 6.6 illustrate that $\dot{V}O_2$ and $\dot{V}CO_2$ are higher for 100 than 50 rpm at all submaximal exercise intensity levels (p < 0.01). The differences seem to decrease at higher exercise intensities.

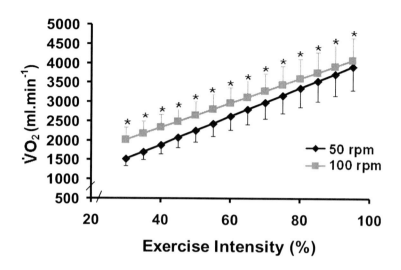

Figure 6.5 V̇O₂ at submaximal intensities for 100 vs. 50 rpm. *Significantly higher than 50 rpm.

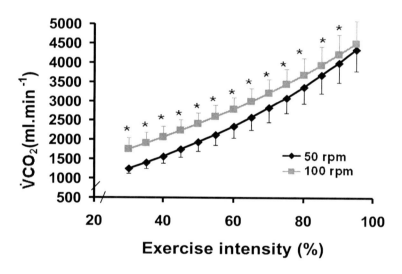

Figure 6.6 V̇CO₂ at submaximal intensities for 100 vs. 50 rpm. *Significantly higher than 50 rpm.

The three parameters describing BLC were not different for 50 and 100 rpm (Table D8, Appendix D). BLC levels were higher ($p < 0.01$) at 100 than 50 rpm at all submaximal intensities (Figure 6.7). Similarly RPY was higher at 100 than 50 rpm at all intensities up to 75% peak power.

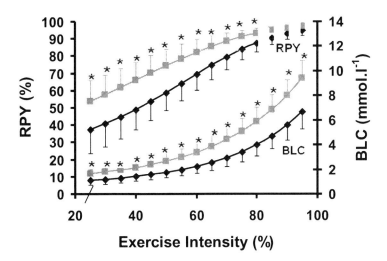

Figure 6.7 BLC and RPY at submaximal intensities for 100 vs. 50 rpm. *Significantly higher than 50 rpm.

However, kel was not different between 50 and 100 rpm 2.25 ± 1.10 vs. 2.42 ± 1.15 $(mmol.l^{-1})^2$, (Figure 6.8). Individual kel values are displayed in appendix D (Table D1).

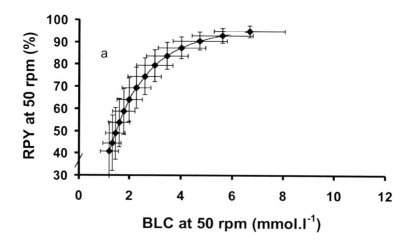

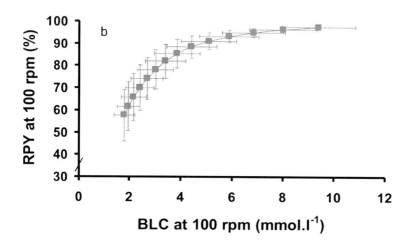

Figure 6.8. The interrelationship between BLC and RPY at 50 (a), and 100 (b).

Furthermore, there was a significant correlation in kel at 50 and 100 rpm (Figure 6.9).

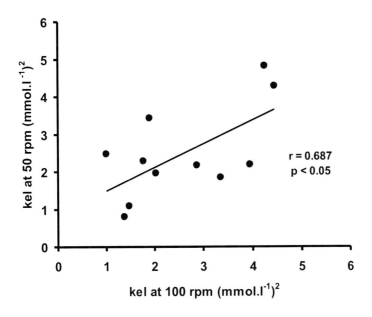

Figure 6.9. Moderate correlation between kel at 50 and 100 rpm.

Absolute rates of CHO were higher at 100 than 50 rpm at all exercise intensities up to 80% of peak power. Conversely, fat oxidation was lower at intensities between 40-65% of peak power (Figure 6.10). This included lower ($p < 0.01$) intensities at Fatmax of 32.7 ± 12.1 vs. 42.7 ± 6.1%, corresponding to (0.43 ± 0.19 vs. 0.53 ± 0.15 g.min^{-1}) for 100 and 50 rpm respectively (Figure 6.10, right panel).

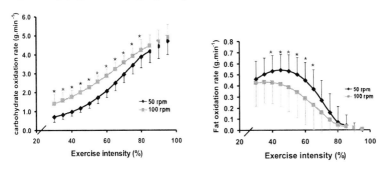

Figure 6.10 Absolute CHO (left panel) and fat (right panel) data at submaximal intensities for 100, and 50 rpm. *Significantly higher RPY, and lower fat at 100 than 50 rpm.

The exercise intensities corresponding to 90% of RPY saturation were significantly higher (p < 0.001) at 100 than at 50 rpm (84.6 ± 7.6 vs. 71.1 ± 10.0) % respectively. However, BLC levels at 90% of RPY were not different for 100 and 50 rpm (4.7±1.7 vs. 4.6 ± 1.2 mmol.l^{-1}) respectively, with a minimum of 2.7 and 3.0, and a maximum of 6.3 and 6.6 mmol.l^{-1}, for 100 and 50 rpm respectively. Exercise intensities at 90% of RPY saturation correlated significantly with kel at 100 rpm (r = 0.687, p < 0.05) but not at 50 rpm (r = 0.565, p = 0.07), (Figure 6.11).

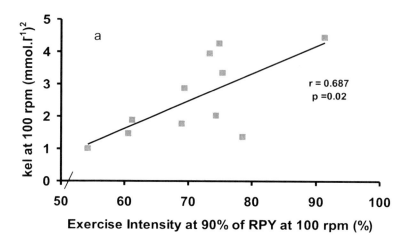

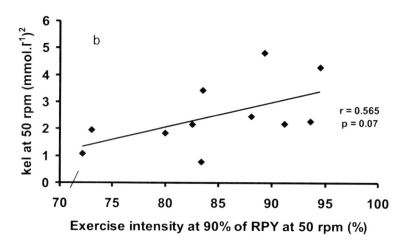

Figure 6.11. Significant correlation between exercise intensities at 90% of RPY saturation at 100 rpm (a), but not at 50 rpm (b).

6.4. DISCUSSION:

The essential finding of this study is that the BLC-RPY interrelationship was unaffected by different pedalling rates, which confirms our hypothesis. Pedalling rate increase from 50 to 100 rpm increased both BLC and RPY (Figure 6.7), without changing the interrelationship between the two (Figure 6.8a, b). Levels of kel (Table D1, Appendix D) are in line with previous suggested values (Beneke 2003b; Beneke 2003a), and are close to what was reported for a similar protocol (Chapter 3). Higher pedalling rate of 100 versus 50 rpm, increased levels of BLC at all submaximal exercise intensities, which is in agreement with previously reported data for similar protocols (Zoladz et al. 2000; Zoladz et al. 2002; Alkhatib et al. 2005). Pedalling rate increase from 50 to 100, also increased absolute and relative rates of CHO, and reduction in fat utilisation at most submaximal exercise intensities suggesting a reduction in the intensity where maximal fat oxidation occur without affecting peak performance.

In chapter 3, BLC changes reflected RPY changes as indicated by levels of kel. The present findings show that BLC seems to reflect the pedalling rate dependent differences in RPY. At any given BLC level, RPY was more or less similar (Figure 6.8a, b), suggesting that pyruvate and lactate are regulated similarly irrespective of cadence.

The pedalling rates of 50 and 100 elicited differences in $\dot{V}O_2$, $\dot{V}CO_2$, and RPY. Those differences seem to diminish at higher intensities as clearly shown (Figures 6.1, 6.2, 6.4, 6.5, 6.6) while BLC differences increase (Figure 6.3, 6.7). The range of BLC levels of approximately 2 - 6 mmol.l^{-1} seem to reflect those differences (Figure 6.7). This is in agreement with our previously published work (Alkhatib et al. 2005), showing that given BLC levels of 2 - 8 mmol.l^{-1} reflected differences in power output and exercise intensity induced by different pedalling rates. The present study suggests that the pedalling rate dependent differences in RPY may be better detectable at given BLC levels rather than at a given exercise intensities.

The present data demonstrated no difference in peak power (Table 6.1) between 50 and 100 rpm, which agrees with incremental testing data reported for 40 versus 100 rpm in Zoladz et al. (2000), and for 50 versus 90 rpm reported in Hughes et al. (1982). The present finding suggests that pedalling rate dependent differences in BLC, and RPY do not necessarily coincide with differences in peak power.

On the other hand, peak BLC was higher for 100 than 50 rpm but surprisingly this was coupled with no change in peak RQ. Higher cadence increased $\dot{V}O_2$ at all submaximal intensities up to 95% (Figure 6.5), and $\dot{V}CO_2$ up to 90% (Figure 6.6). However, an additional $\dot{V}CO_2$ induced by increased bicarbonate buffering (Jeukendrup and Wallis 2005) at maximal intensity levels for both 50 and 100 rpm may explain no difference in $\dot{V}CO_2$ at intensities above 90%. The in the cadence induced differences on $\dot{V}O_2$, and on $\dot{V}CO_2$ were systematically diminished at peak levels (Figure 6.5, 6.6). This may be explained by similar increase in breathing frequency and minute ventilation which has been reported not to be different at maximal intensities in spite of different cadence (Chavarren and Calbet 1999). Therefore, at peak level, the combined latter effects on $\dot{V}O_2$, and $\dot{V}CO_2$ may explain the similar RQ (Table 6.1).

Pedalling rate effects on exercise performance are governed by many physiological factors that varied from a change in muscle fibre recruitment patterns (Pringle *et al.* 2003; Ahlquist *et al.* 1992), mechanical and energy efficiency (Gaesser and Brooks 1975), and neuromuscular fatigue (Takaishi *et al.* 1996). Those studies have reported higher BLC at higher pedalling rate for a given power output or exercise intensity. The mechanisms for this increase are not fully understood. Studies linking pedalling rate dependent differences on BLC with muscle fibre recruitment types proved paradoxical (Ahlquist *et al.* 1992 in Denadai *et al.* 2006). Denadai *et al.* (2006) suggested that increased pedalling rate seems to influence the lactate response to exercise, increasing the energy demand at the highest pedalling rate, and suggesting causative effects of BLC on fuel mix. However, these suggestions were based only on reported BLC response. Chavarren and Calbet (1999) reported that the relationship between BLC and $\dot{V}O_2$ is independent of cadence, indicating that it may be related to energy expenditure. This was supported by the present study showing that at any level of BLC, RPY is unaffected by cadence suggesting that the BLC-RPY interrelationship is also independent of cadence. This can be explained by that kel seem to indicate the combustion of relative fat and CHO at any rate of production, or at any level of BLC.

Maximal lactate steady state (MLSS) is the highest BLC that can be maintained over time without continual blood lactate accumulation (Beneke 2003a). MLSS has recently been shown to be independent of pedalling rate (Denadai *et al.* 2006). The latter study has also reported higher intensities at MLSS at 50 than 100 rpm, without any change in MLSS. We have suggested in chapter 3, that BLC levels at approximately 90% of RPY saturation, measured during incremental test, correspond to MLSS. Since the present study showed higher exercise intensities, coupled with no difference in BLC levels, at 90% of RPY at 50 than 100 rpm, it is possible to suggest that BLC levels at 90% reflect MLSS independence of pedalling rate.

We detected approximately 14% higher exercise intensity at 90% RPY at 50 than 100 rpm. This is in line with a 10% higher exercise intensity at MLSS at 50 than 100 rpm reported in Denadai *et al.* (2006). Furthermore, the present data also showed a positive correlation (p < 0.05) between the intensities at 90% RPY and individual kel values at 100 rpm (Figure 6.9). This confirms that kel individual values may help to detect MLSS and exercise performance at MLSS, irrespective of pedalling rate.

The present finding shows that higher cadence increases the rate of CHO oxidation at almost all submaximal exercise intensities, which is consistent with higher CHO oxidation previously reported at a higher cadence at various exercise intensities (Kang *et al.* 2004; Gaesser and Brooks 1975; McDaniel *et al.* 2002). Fat oxidation was lowered as pedalling rate increased especially at intensities between 40-60% of peak power. These intensities correspond to those where fat oxidation is maximal (Achten and Jeukendrup 2003; Venables *et al.* 2005). This was confirmed as we found approximately 23% lower Fatmax and 10% lower intensity at Fatmax at 100 compared with 50 rpm. Pedalling rate induced alterations on Fatmax, and Fatmax intensity may be important as a limiting factor to exercise performance at prolonged endurance events due to glycogen depletion mechanisms (Ball *et al.* 1995; Below *et al.* 1995; Hargreaves 2004).

Furthermore, the latter cadence effects on Fatmax and the Fatmax intensity did not affect peak power, suggesting that alterations in Fatmax do not necessarily affect peak performance.

6.4.1. Methodological aspects:

Low pedalling rate i.e. 50 rpm has long been used in protocols estimating (Swain and Wright 1997) or predicting $\dot{V}O_{2peak}$ (Astrand and Ryhming 1954), and has been reported not to be different from 80 rpm (Swain and Wright 1997). This study selected 50 and 100 rpm to show several effects on the BLC-RPY interrelationship. However, it cannot rule out that higher or lower pedalling rate effects on the latter interrelationship may still require further research.

It is agreed that the optimal cadence is between 60-80 rpm in terms of the metabolic efficiency (Foss & Hallen 2004). Highly trained athletes are known to prefer high cadence between 90-100 rpm (Hagberg *et al.* 1981), but patients prefer low cadence (Sargent *et al.* 2002). Thus, this study cannot rule out that homogeneity of out subjects may have affected our results. However, the correlation found (Figure 6.9), clearly support that individual kel values are not affected by cadence.

Based on the present data we may suggest a preference of cycling at a lower cadence as it burns more fat at the same given exercise intensity. However, further testing may be required with a different protocol to confirm the latter effects during training, and with a clinical special population.

6.5. CONCLUSION

Increasing pedalling rate increases CHO, and reduces fat utilisation at almost all intensity levels, especially at lower exercise intensities. Pedalling rate increase from 50 to 100 rpm increased both levels of BLC and RPY but did not affect the interrelationship between the two as indicated by kel values. Changes in BLC levels indicated RPY changes, irrespective of cadence. Thus, pyruvate and lactate are regulated similarly irrespective of cadence.

These effects of modes of exercise on pyruvate and fat metabolism suggest a practical importance in sport events where substrate utilisation control is a limiting factor. It may also be important in clinical and exercise prescription and obesity control, where the ability to oxidise fat matters.

CHAPTER SEVEN

THE EFFECTS OF HANDLEBAR GRIPPING ON THE BLC-RPY INTERRELATIONSHIP

7.1. INTRODUCTION

Different modes of exercise i.e. cycling vs. running, low vs. high cadence, or handgrip vs. non-grip cycling, have been shown to induce differences on power output and responses of BLC, $\dot{V}O_2$, and $\dot{V}CO_2$ (Billat *et al.* 2000; Caputo and Denadai 2006; Baker *et al.* 2002).

Different muscle mass has been shown to be responsible for differences in BLC induced by different exercise modes (Beneke and vonDuvillard 1996). These effects on BLC have also been reported after a 20-s supramaximal cycling exercise (Baker *et al.* 2002). The latter reported higher BLC in the 4th min of recovery when gripping the bicycle handlebar (HG) compared with a non-gripping (NG) protocol. Higher BLC in HG protocol has been explained by higher muscle mass contribution from the forearm muscles (Baker *et al.* 2002). Higher peak, and mean power in HG vs. NG has also been reported for a similar protocol in male and female teenagers (Dore *et al.* 2006). Males have demonstrated higher power output than females, which have been attributed to a higher fat free muscle mass contribution from the upper body.

The $\dot{V}O_2$ responses to maximal and submaximal exercise have been shown to be affected by additional light arm cranking, to leg incremental cycling (Billat *et al.* 2000). However, it is not clear whether the latter effects are reflected on the overall body fuel mix. No study has investigated whether increased muscle mass induced by HG has any effect on the relative rates of CHO and fat utilisation.

Whole body fat and CHO utilisation has recently been shown to be affected by different muscle mass induced by different modes of exercise i.e. cycling vs. Triathlon (Gonzalez-Haro *et al.* 2007). However, those changes in the local working muscles are not always reflected on the whole body level. Recent reports suggested that local muscle fat oxidation is regulated by the overall body and not local muscle mass (Nordby *et al.* 2006). This group of investigators found that leg muscles oxidative capacity, as measured by enzymatic activities in a muscle biopsy, was not correlated with whole body $\dot{V}O_{2peak}$;

Whereas, whole body fat oxidation did. It is unknown to what extent a small difference in muscle mass involved in an exercise such as HG vs. NG would alter whole body CHO and fat utilisation.

Using several exercise modalities, Beneke (2003b) demonstrated that MLSS depends on several factors such as cardiac output, body mass, pyruvate utilisation expressed as kel, and relative muscle mass. Beneke (2003b) suggested that an increase in relative muscle mass is likely to increases BLC response at the same intensity. An increase in muscle mass involved in an exercise would also increase $\dot{V}O_2$ (Billat et al. 2000), and probably increase $\dot{V}CO_2$, and therefore BLC-RPY interrelationship.

Previously (Chapter 6), it has been found that BLC-RPY interrelationship was not affected by muscle contraction frequency induced by different pedalling rates. BLC levels indicate RPY irrespective of cadence. This study investigates whether a change in muscle mass induced by gripping the handlebar affects BLC-RPY interrelationship expressed as kel.

We hypothesize that RPY is regulated by the availability of pyruvate as indicated by BLC irrespective of muscle mass.

7.2. METHODS

Eleven healthy male subjects (age: 30.5 ± 5.6 years, height 179.8 ± 6.7 cm, body mass: 73.4 ± 8.5 kg) completed two separate incremental load step cycling tests to exhaustion within a period of two weeks. Both tests were performed at similar time of the test day, in random order. The same electrically braked cycle Ergometer, (Lode Excalibur Sport, the Netherlands) was used for each test. Seat and handle bar height and angle were recorded for the first test and reproduced for the subsequent test.

The HG protocol involved the subjects placing their hands upon the handlebars of the cycle ergometer in a normal gripping fashion. The NG protocol consisted of the subjects relaxing their arms to the side of the upper body. In the NG condition, the subjects were instructed to limit the torso flexion as much as possible.

The power output was initiated to correspond to 0.5 W.kg^{-1} body mass, and increased by 0.5 W.kg^{-1} body mass every 2-min stage. Blood samples were drawn from the hyperaemic earlobe at the end of eachstage, and analysed for lactate as described in the general methods (Chapter 2). $\dot{V}O_2$ and $\dot{V}CO_2$ samples were collected and analysed as described in the general methods section (Chapter 2).

Relative exercise intensities were calculated as a percentage of peak power, and determined as explained in (Chapter 3). RPY was estimated from $\dot{V}O_2$ and $\dot{V}CO_2$ using indirect calorimetry, and further described as a sigmoid function of BLC as described in (Chapter 3). Furthermore, $\dot{V}O_2$, $\dot{V}CO_2$, and BLC data were fitted using linear and nonlinear regression models as described in chapter 3.

Descriptive data were presented as mean ± SD. Differences between the two protocols rates were tested using repeated measures ANOVA, and Bonferroni post hoc test. Correlations were tested using Pearson's product of moment test.

7.3. RESULTS

Peak power was significantly higher ($p < 0.05$) at HG than NG (Table 7.1). However, peak BLC, $\dot{V}O_2$, and $\dot{V}CO_2$, and RQ were not different (Table 7.1).

Peak data	Handgrip	Non-grip
Power (W)	300.8 ± 50.5	286.2 ± 46.1*
BLC mmol.l^{-1}	10.8 ± 2.7	10.2 ± 3.0
$\dot{V}O_2$ ml.min^{-1}	3823 ± 618	3813 ± 625
$\dot{V}CO_2$ ml.min^{-1}	4515 ± 789	4267 ± 663 (p=0.096)
RQ	1.15 ± 0.07	1.12 ± 0.04

Table 7.1. Peak data for HG and NG protocols. *Significantly lower than HG.

$\dot{V}O_2$ was increased ($p < 0.05$) almost linearly by 413 ± 34 and 457 ± 48 ml.min^{-1} every stage for HG and NG respectively. $\dot{V}O_2$ was not different at low power outputs, but was higher for NG than HG at all power outputs higher than 147.6 ± 15.8 W ($p < 0.01$), (Figure 7.1).

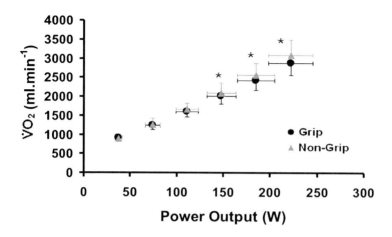

Figure 7.1 Submaximal $\dot{V}O_2$ data for mean stages completed by all subjects for HG and NG protocols. *Significantly higher in NG than HG

Similarly, $\dot{V}CO_2$ was increased ($p < 0.05$) by 493 ± 89 and 551 ± 93 ml.min^{-1} every stage for HG and NG respectively. $\dot{V}CO_2$ was higher at NG than HG at higher power outputs than 147.6 ± 15.8 W ($p < 0.01$), (Figure 7.2).

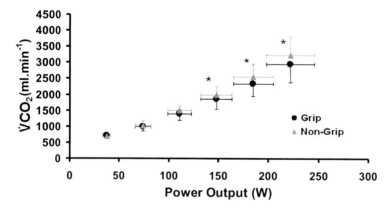

Figure 7.2. Submaximal $\dot{V}CO_2$ data for mean stages completed by all subjects for HG and NG protocols. *Significantly higher in NG than HG.

BLC increased progressively ($p < 0.05$) in both HG and NG. The increase became progressively steeper ($p < 0.05$) above stage 5 corresponding to power output of 184.6 ± 19.8 W and exercise intensities of 62.5 ± 10 % (Figure 7.3). BLC levels were not different at power outputs below 221.5 ± 23.8 corresponding to 4.0 ± 2.1 mmol.l^{-1}. At and above that level, BLC was higher at NG than HG at this level ($p < 0.05$), (Figure 7.3).

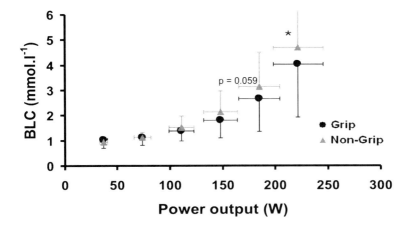

Figure 7.3. Submaximal BLC data for mean stages completed by all subjects for HG and NG protocols. *Significantly higher in NG than HG.

RPY increased continuously ($p < 0.05$) for both HG and NG, but the increase started to diminish at stage 3 and above corresponding to a power output of 110.7 ± 11.9 W and exercise intensity of 37.5 ± 5.9 % (Figure 7.4).

RPY was not different at low power outputs, but was higher for NG than HG at higher power outputs than 147.6 ± 15.8 W, corresponding to RPY of 66.3 ± 20.0 vs. 80.9 ± 15.4% for HG and NG respectively ($p < 0.01$), (Figure 7.4).

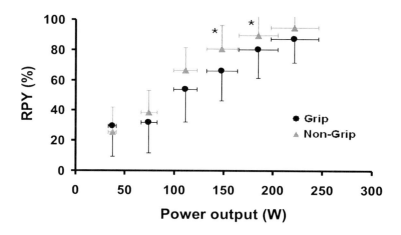

Figure 7.4. Submaximal RPY data for mean stages completed by all subjects for HG and NG protocols. *Significantly higher in NG than HG.

The coefficient of determination for the fitted submaximal data of $\dot{V}O_2$, $\dot{V}CO_2$ and BLC at given exercise intensities were (0.995 ± 0.003, 0.998 ± 0.002 and 0.997 ± 0.005) in HG, and (0.994 ± 0.003, 0.998 ± 0.001 and 0.997 ± 0.005) in NG, respectively ($p < 0.001$).

Figure 7.5 illustrates that there are no differences induced by different gripping on BLC and RPY at all submaximal exercise intensities.

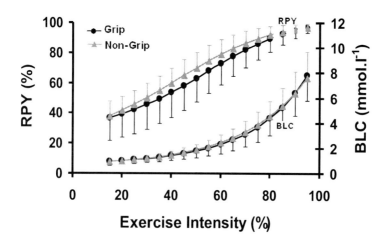

Figure 7.5. Effects of HG versus NG protocols on BLC, and RPY.

kel was not different between HG and NG, 1.694 ± 0.618 vs. 1.445 ± 0.426 $(mmol.l^{-1})^2$, (Figure 7.6). Individual levels of kel are displayed in appendix E (Table E1).

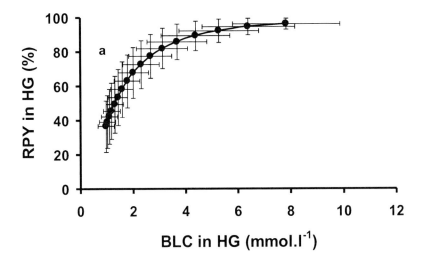

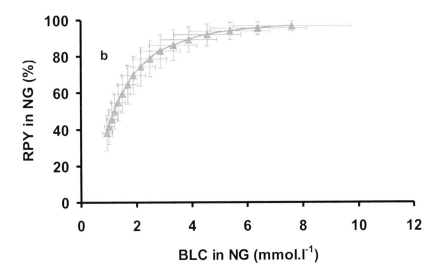

Figure 7.6. RPY as a function of BLC in HG (a) and NG (b) protocols.

However, there was no kel correlation between HG and NG.

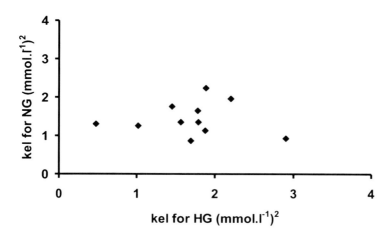

Figure 7.7. No correlation between kel for HG and NG protocols.

7.4. DISCUSSION

The main finding of this study is that handgrip induced metabolic changes in muscle mass reflected on BLC and RPY did not change the interrelationship between the two as indicated by kel. The present study suggests that local muscle RPY contribution from HG did not affect the overall RPY, which is reflected by unchanged levels of BLC (Figure 7.5). Unchanged kel levels seem to suggest that BLC-RPY interrelationship independent of muscle mass induced changes by HG and NG protocols (Figure 7.6). This supports previous findings in this book (Chapter 6) relating to the BLC-RPY interrelationship is independent of different muscle contraction frequency induced by different pedalling rates. The results of the present study may suggest that BLC-RPY is independent of muscle mass. However, the lack of correlation between kel of HG and NG protocols (Figure 7.7) suggests that the study design may have affected the assumption of induced different muscle mass. Higher $\dot{V}O_2$, $\dot{V}CO_2$, BLC, and RPY at given power outputs in NG than HG (Figures 7.1, 7.2, 7.3, 7.4) suggests that higher muscle mass was induced by NG than that induced by HG.

There is no previous research about the possible effects of muscle mass on the BLC-RPY interrelationship, and whether changes in BLC could reflect changes in RPY. Chudalla *et al.* (2006) suggested local and systematic effects on BLC during exercise with small and larger muscle groups, regardless of oxygen tension (PO_2). Others indicated that smaller muscle mass contribution, from the arm cranking to the whole body (arm and leg cranking and cycling), induced higher $\dot{V}O_2$ slow components, and $\dot{V}O_{2peak}$, without affecting BLC threshold (defined as $\dot{V}O_2$ corresponding to the starting point of an accelerated lactate accumulation in the range of 3-5 mmol.l^{-1}) (Billat *et al.* 2000). The present data support the latter finding, and illustrated no difference in kel (Figure 7.5). The reported BLC-threshold (3-5 mmol.l^{-1}) in Billat *et al.* (2000) is expected to reflect 90% of RPY (Chapter 3). As kel depends on both BLC, and RPY, unchanged BLC is expected to reflect unchanged RPY. This suggests that the BLC-RPY interrelationship is independent of changes in muscle mass fuel mix induced by handgrip.

Handlebar gripping is used during cycling to stabilise the upper body and focus the force on the legs towards achieving the desired mechanical power. Baker *et al.* (2002) explained that by pulling upon the handlebar, the centre of mass of the whole body is maintained at a constant vertical position level, so the leg extension can be directed to pushing down the pedals. Therefore, it is unsurprising that higher peak power is found in HG than in NG in the present data, which agrees with previously reported data of supramaximal exercise (Baker *et al.* 2002). The higher peak power in the HG than NG, with no difference in $\dot{V}O_{2peak}$ reflects a higher work efficiency in HG than NG at higher absolute workload (Table 7.1). This is reflected by a difference of 0.6 ml.min.W^{-1} equivalent to approximately 5% added energy at NG to achieve the same workload.

Torso movement during cycling exercise has been suggested to affect indirect calorimetry and energy expenditure (McDaniel *et al.* 2005), though the effects on $\dot{V}O_2$, or gross mechanical efficiency are less apparent (Low and Coast, 1991 in McDaniel *et al.* 2005). The contribution can be 1-2% higher when the torso is moving than when it is fixed , especially at low pedalling rate i.e. 40rpm (McDaniel *et al.* 2005). In the present study, the torso movement may have affected the present results, especially with the used pedalling rate of 50 rpm. This may have been reflected by higher $\dot{V}O_2$, and $\dot{V}CO_2$ (Figures 7.1, 7.2), and higher BLC and RPY at the same workloads, but not intensities (Figure 7.5) in NG than in HG protocol. These effects were observed especially at workloads higher than approximately 150 W. The increased workload requires increased muscular effort in the arms and torso to remain in position on the ergometer saddle. This had to be compensated by increased torso movement at higher workloads observed in the NG protocol. This suggests that NG protocol may have demonstrated higher muscle mass contribution than HG. However, our data have also shown that at any given intensity no effects were seen on RPY which is indicated by no change in BLC (Figure 7.5). Hence, those effects of torso movement are not likely to have influenced the BLC-RPY interrelationship.

It is not yet agreed whether changes in whole body fat and CHO utilisation are also due to the local working muscle substrate utilisation, though many researchers assume that changes in whole-body respiration are due to the respiration in the working muscles (Sidossis *et al.* 1992; Coyle *et al.* 1992; Chavarren and Calbet 1999; Horowitz *et al.* 1994; McDaniel *et al.* 2002; in McDaniel *et al.* 2005). However, leg oxidative capacity as measured in muscle biopsies by enzymatic activities of citrate synthase and Hydroxy-acyle-CoA-dehydrogenase has been found independent of whole body substrate oxidation reflected as Fatmax (Nordby *et al.* 2006). This has occurred in spite of correlation between $\dot{V}O_{2peak}$ and whole body peak fat oxidation, suggesting that leg muscle oxidative capacity is not the main determinant of whole-body fat oxidation in healthy subjects. In the present study this may suggest that the small changes at local muscle level induced by HG may have not been significant enough to alter whole body fat and CHO utilisation.

The BLC-RPY interrelationship is based on whole body measurements of BLC and RPY. BLC measured via capillary is known to represent whole body blood lactate (Langlands and Wallace, 1965; cited in Robergs *et al.* 1991), and that RPY estimates at given intensities are based on indirect calorimetry. Thus, it is expected that no change in BLC levels would indicate no change in RPY (Figure 7.5).

The contribution of a small muscle mass, induced by HG, or NG, affects neither relative, nor absolute rates of whole body fat, or CHO oxidation if related to exercise intensity (Table E3, E4, Appendix E). This suggests that regardless of oxygen availability, the availability of pyruvate influence the RPY (Spriet and Heigenhauser 2002), hence, CHO, and fat utilisation, which is in line with the notion considering CHO metabolism as the main regulator of fat metabolism (Sidossis *et al.* 1997; Coyle *et al.* 1997).

7.4.1. Limitation:

The lack of correlation between kel for HG and NG coupled with very similar values of kel suggest that alterations in local muscle groups induced by the HG and NG protocols may have altered various physiological parameters such as BLC and RPY differently without affecting kel (Table 7.2). This may be illustrated by a higher RPY at stage 4, and 5 (Figure 7.4), and higher BLC only in stage 5 (Figure 7.3).

The present study does not rule out a potential difference in fibre composition when using HG, and NG protocols. It has been reported that arms have higher proportion of type-II muscle fibres than legs in the same subject (Billat *et al.* 2000). Fast twitch muscle fibres have lower contractile-coupling frequency, and greater energy cost to perform a standardised contraction. However, whether the latter difference in the upper body reflect differences in whole body RPY, or BLC remains inconclusive (Sawka 1986).

Upper body exercise has been reported to elicit higher indirect calorimetry, and possibly BLC at given power output than lower body cycling, due to a lower muscle mass in the upper limbs (Sawka 1986). However, the present protocol may have not triggered enough different muscle mass. While higher contribution of muscle mass is expected for the HG (Baker *et al.* 2002), effects of torso movement may have contributed adversely, reducing the effects of HG especially for given exercise intensities (Figure 7.5). Future research may consider different protocols that trigger higher differences in muscle mass.

7.5. CONCLUSION

NG affected BLC, $\dot{V}O_2$, $\dot{V}CO_2$, and RPY at given workload, but has no effects at given intensities. At any given BLC level, RPY was also unchanged, and both unaffected by different protocols of HG and NG. The BLC-RPY interrelationship may be independent of HG and NG induced changes in muscle mass. However, the chosen protocols of HG vs. NG did not reflect the expected change muscle mass. Future studies may consider choosing different study design to allow bigger differences in muscle mass.

CHAPTER EIGHT

CONCLUSION

The main finding of this book is that the sigmoid interrelationship between BLC and RPY can be used to characterise changes between the two during exercise. The studies within this book established the BLC-RPY interrelationship and tested it against data sampling and processing procedure and variations in exercise protocol, modes and duration. This was established with respect to studies reporting that pyruvate availability is one of the main determinants of RPY, and that CHO availability controls fat oxidation (Coyle *et al.* 1988, Hargreaves and Spriet 2005, Spriet *et al.* 2000, Spriet and Heigenhauser 2002, Mourtazakis *et al.* 2006), capillary BLC represents whole body arterial blood lactate (Langlands and Wallace 1965; in Robergs *et al.* 1991), and that the main fate of BLC during exercise is oxidation via its conversion to pyruvate (Brooks *et al.* 2005). However, different interpretations of the regulatory mechanisms of RPY and BLC are acknowledged (Chapter 1).

Initially we established the BLC-RPY interrelationship in incremental cycle ergometer testing (Chapter 3), and found that individual kel levels of approximately 0.5 - 5 $(mmol.l^{-1})^2$ explained changes in RPY. Subsequent chapters (Table 8.1) demonstrated similar range of kel, which is in agreement with values theoretically modelled, or observed for healthy subjects previously (Mader and Heck 1986, Beneke 2003a, b). The latter values may also serve to indicate levels of MLSS which vary between 2 - 7 $mmol.l^{-1}$ (Beneke 2000, Billat 2003). Levels of kel may be useful indicators of inter-individual variability in fat and CHO utilisation, and can be useful indicators of differences between exercise intensities corresponding to Fatmax and the cross-point observed in a small group size (Stephens *et al.* 2006), or large group size (Venables *et al.* 2005).

Based on the onset kinetics and the adaptation of $\dot{V}O_2$ and $\dot{V}CO_2$, we demonstrated that averaging period affected the BLC-RPY interrelationship (Chapter 4). Extending the averaging period to include a whole stage of 2-min compared with the last 60- or 30-s induced differential decreases in $\dot{V}O_2$ and in $\dot{V}CO_2$ respectively. This caused underestimation of RPY and overestimation of RFAT during exercise, characterised by small but significant increase in kel. This suggested using the last 30-s of a 2-min stage as an appropriate averaging method for indirect calorimetry, and for estimating levels of kel.

Furthermore, longer stage duration protocol induced unchanged kel between protocols (Chapter 5), though within protocol data suggest a more accurate estimation of kel if duration is > 4 min. We observed adverse effects on BLC and RPY caused by using different protocols, limiting the sensitivity of kel in detecting duration changes. Within protocol comparisons of the 2nd, 4th, and 6th min elicited no kel difference but better kel correlation between 4th and 6th than 2nd and 6th min within a 6-min protocol (Chapter 5). The latter suggested a stage duration of at least 4-min and above for $\dot{V}O_2$, $\dot{V}CO_2$, and BLC kinetics, and for a better description of the BLC-RPY interrelationship.

To investigate the effects of modes of exercise, we selected pedalling rate as a representative of muscle contraction frequency (Chapter 6), and handlebar gripping as a representative of increasing muscle mass (Chapter 7). The pedalling rate dependent differences induced on BLC and RPY did not affect the interrelationship between the two as indicated by indifferent kel values. This suggests that any change in BLC levels indicates RPY changes, irrespective of cadence. Similarly the BLC-RPY interrelationship was independent of HG, and NG induced changes in muscle mass. NG protocol induced higher RPY, and BLC at given workloads, but affected neither at given exercise intensities. No difference in BLC at given intensity indicated no RPY difference, as indicated by similar kel levels. This suggests that central mechanisms of whole body CHO and fat utilisation are not significantly influenced by changes at the muscle local levels induced by handgrip in agreement with recent findings (Nordby *et al.* 2006). This confirms that modes of exercise do not affect the BLC-RPY interrelationship. Any change in RPY will be indicated by levels of BLC.

Practical use of Levels of kel may serve as good indicator of individual's RPY, and RFAT, and therefore, may be useful in sport events where substrate utilisation control is a limiting factor. It may also be useful in clinical and exercise prescription and obesity control, where the ability to oxidize fat matters. kel may be useful in indicating MLSS levels. The latter proved beneficial in training as previously shown (Billat 2004). However, further testing on kel is required to provide a meaningful use in training.

8.1. LIMITATIONS

The BLC-RPY model is based on the assumption that RPY is determined by the availability of pyruvate, suggesting that pyruvate is the most important factor (Chapter 1). However, this has not been established yet, and current research still suggests conflicting data in this regard (Chapter 1).

The current BLC-RPY model examines all exercise intensities when RQ ≤ 1. Levels of BLC indicate RPY as reflected by kel estimates. However, these are only meaningful where used in conjunction with indirect calorimetry when RQ ≤ 1. When RPY reaches near 100% an excess non-oxidative CO_2, and elevates $\dot{V}CO_2$, which possibly overestimates CHO, and underestimates fat oxidation (Jeukendrup and Wallis 2005).

Results of chapter 7 suggest that BLC-RPY interrelationship is not affected by HG vs. NG. However, the latter testing protocol probably did not test the muscle mass effects. Different protocols i.e. upright vs. recumbent cycling may be introduced in the future to investigate the effects of muscle mass.

Incremental testing has its own limitation starting from failing to achieve a prolonged steady state, which requires longer exercise durations. The number of stages achieved at an incremental test is crucial in estimating kel but some individuals do not achieve enough stages below RQ ≤ 1 where indirect calorimetry is valid. Longer stage duration protocols may be favourable for achieving a steady state but do not elicit enough data points below RQ =1. Based on the previous chapter we suggested a protocol with at least 4-min stage duration.

The present work suggests that the BLC-RPY can be characterised by levels of kel. The work also shows the test protocol describing this interrelation needs to consider several factors in terms of design and interpretation which can influence the estimation of kel. The table below (Table 8.1) summarises the latter effects on levels of kel as investigated within chapters of this book.

Chapter no	Subject No	Protocol	kel $(mmol.l^{-1})^2$ Mean ± SD	p-value
3	21	2-min stages 50 rpm 1 increased by 0.5 W.kg^{-1}	1.82 ± 0.95 $r^2 = 0.86$	___
4	21	2-min stages 50 rpm 1 increased by 0.5 W.kg^{-1} Averaging the last 30, 60- or 120 of a stage	1.82 ± 0.95 for 30 2.22 ± 1.23 for 60 2.57 ± 1.43 for 120 s	< 0.01
5	11	2-min stages 50-rpm and 6-min stages 50-rpm 0.5 increased by 0.5 W.kg^{-1}	1.24 ± 0.52 for 2-min 1.16 ± 0.79 for 6-min	N.S
5	11	6-min stages using the 2nd, 4th, and 6th min. 0.5 increased by 0.5 W.kg^{-1}	1.56 ± 1.2 for 2nd, 1.22 ± 0.78 for 4th, 1.16 ± 0.79 for 6th min.	N.S
6	11	2-min stages 50 and 100 rpm 1 increased by 0.5 W.kg^{-1}	2.25 ± 1.10 at 50 vs. 2.42 ± 1.15 at 100 rpm	N.S
7	11	2-min stages 50-rpm for HG and NG 0.5 increased by 0.5 W.kg^{-1}	1.69 ± 0.62 for HG vs. 1.45 ± 0.43 for NG	N.S

Table 8.1 Effects of variations in exercise protocol, modes and duration on kel values

CHAPTER NINE

REFERENCES

Achten, J., Gleeson, M. and Jeukendrup, A. E. (2002) Determination of the exercise intensity that elicits maximal fat oxidation. *Medicine and Science in Sports and Exercise*, 34, 92-97.

Achten, J. and Jeukendrup, A. E. (2003) Maximal fat oxidation during exercise in trained men. *International Journal of Sports Medicine*, 24, 603-608.

Achten, J. and Jeukendrup, A. E. (2004) Relation between plasma lactate concentration and fat oxidation rates over a wide range of exercise intensities. *International Journal of Sports Medicine*, 25, 32-37.

Ahlquist, L. E., Bassett, D. R., Jr., Sufit, R., Nagle, F. J. and Thomas, D. P. (1992) The effect of pedaling frequency on glycogen depletion rates in type I and type II quadriceps muscle fibers during submaximal cycling exercise. *European Journal of Applied Physiology and Occupational Physiology*, 65, 360-364.

Alkhatib, A. and Beneke, R. (2005) Description of the blood lactate concentration to incremental exercise using 2- & 3-parameter models. *European College of Sport Science*, Book of abstracts, 232.

Alkhatib, A., von Duvillard, S. P. and Beneke, R. (2005) Effects of Cycling Cadence on Workload and Relative Intensity at given Blood lactate Concentration. *Medicine and Science in Sport and Exercise*, 37, S104.

ASTRAND, P. O. and RYHMING, I. (1954) A nomogram for calculation of aerobic capacity (physical fitness) from pulse rate during submaximal work. *Journal of Applied Physiology*, 7, 218-221.

Baker, J., Brown, E., Hill, G., Phillips, G., Williams, R. and Davies, B. (2002) Handgrip contribution to lactate production and leg power during high-intensity exercise. *Medicine and Science in Sports and Exercise*, 34, 1037-1040.

Ball, T. C., Headley, S. A., Vanderburgh, P. M. and Smith, J. C. (1995) Periodic carbohydrate replacement during 50 min of high-intensity cycling improves subsequent sprint performance. *International Journal of Sport Nutrition*, 5, 151-158.

Beaver, W. L., Wasserman, K. and Whipp, B. J. (1986) A New Method for Detecting Anaerobic Threshold by Gas-Exchange. *Journal of Applied Physiology*, 60, 2020-2027.

Bell, C., Kowalchuk, J. M., Paterson, D. H., Scheuermann, B. W. and Cunningham, D. A. (1999) The effects of caffeine on the kinetics of O-2 uptake, CO2 production and expiratory ventilation in humans during the on-transient of moderate and heavy intensity exercise. *Experimental Physiology*, 84, 761-774.

Below, P. R., Mora-Rodriguez, R., Gonzalez-Alonso, J. and Coyle, E. F. (1995) Fluid and carbohydrate ingestion independently improve performance during 1 h of intense exercise. *Medicine and Science in Sports and Exercise*, 27, 200-210.

Beneke, R. (2003a) Experiment and computer aided simulation: complementary tools to understand exercise metabolism. *Biochemical Society Transactions*, 31, 1263-1266.

Beneke, R. (2003b) Maximal lactate steady state concentration (MLSS): experimental and modelling approaches. *European Journal of Applied Physiology and Occupational Physiology*, 88, 361-369.

Beneke, R. (2003c) Methodological aspects of maximal lactate steady state-implications for performance testing. *European Journal of Applied Physiology*, 89, 95-99.

Beneke, R., Hutler, M. and Leithauser, R. M. (2000) Maximal lactate-steady-state independent of performance. *Medicine and Science in Sports and Exercise*, 32, 1135-1139.

Beneke, R. and vonDuvillard, S. P. (1996) Determination of maximal lactate steady state response in selected sports events. *Medicine and Science in Sports and Exercise*, 28, 241-246.

Berg, J. M., Tymoczko, J. L. and Stryer, L. (2002) *Biochemistry*. W.H Freeman and Company, USA.

Bergman, B. C. and Brooks, G. A. (1999) Respiratory gas-exchange ratios during graded exercise in fed and fasted trained and untrained men. *Journal of Applied Physiology*, 86, 479-487.

Bergman, B. C., Wolfel, E. E., Butterfield, G. E., Lopaschuk, G. D., Casazza, G. A., Horning, M. A. and Brooks, G. A. (1999) Active muscle and whole body lactate kinetics after endurance training in men. *Journal of Applied Physiology*, 87, 1684-1696.

Bergstrom, J. (1975) Percutaneous Needle-Biopsy of Skeletal-Muscle in Physiological and Clinical Research. *Scandinavian Journal of Clinical & Laboratory Investigation*, 35, 606-616.

Bergstrom, J., Hermansen, L., Hultman, E. and Saltin, B. (1967) Diet, muscle glycogen and physical performance. *Acta Physiologica Scandinavian.*, 71, 140-150.

Billat, V., Sirvent, P., Lepretre, P. M. and Koralsztein, J. P. (2004) Training effect on performance, substrate balance and blood lactate concentration at maximal lactate steady state in master endurance-runners. *Pflugers Archiv.European Journal of Physiology*, 447, 875-883.

Billat, V. L., Hamard, L., Bocquet, V., Demarie, S., Beroni, M., Petit, B. and Koralsztein, J. P. (2000) Influence of light additional arm cranking exercise on the kinetics of VO2 in severe cycling exercise. *International Journal of Sports Medicine*, 21, 344-350.

Billat, V. L., Sirvent, P., Py, G., Koralsztein, J. P. and Mercier, J. (2003) The concept of maximal lactate steady state: a bridge between biochemistry, physiology and sport science. *Sports Medicine*, 33, 407-426.

Bircher, S. and Knechtle, B. (2004) Relationship between fat oxidation and lactate threshold in athletes and obese women and men. *Journal of Sports Science and Medicine*, 3, 174-181.

Bircher, S., Knechtle, B. and Knecht, H. (2005) Is the intensity of the highest fat oxidation at the lactate concentration of 2 mmol L-1? A comparison of two different exercise protocols. *European Journal of Clinical Investigation*, 35, 491-498..

Boning, D. (2001) Differences between whole blood and plasma lactate concentrations have to be considered when comparing various studies. *Medicine and Science in Sports and Exercise*, 33, 1411-1412.

Bourgois, J. and Vrijens, J. (1998) Metabolic and cardiorespiratory responses in young oarsmen during prolonged exercise tests on a rowing ergometer at power outputs corresponding to two concepts of anaerobic threshold. *European Journal of Applied Physiology and Occupational Physiology*, 77, 164-169.

Boyd, A. E., Giamber, S. R., Mager, M. and Lebovitz, H. E. (1974) Lactate Inhibition of Lipolysis in Exercising Man. *Metabolism-Clinical and Experimental*, 23, 531-542.

Brittain, C. J., Rossiter, H. B., Kowalchuk, J. M. and Whipp, B. J. (2001) Effect of prior metabolic rate on the kinetics of oxygen uptake during moderate-intensity exercise. *European Journal of Applied Physiology and Occupational Physiology*, 86, 125-134.

Brooks, G. A. (1985) Anaerobic Threshold - Review of the Concept and Directions for Future-Research. *Medicine and Science in Sports and Exercise*, 17, 22-31.

Brooks, G. A. (1998) Mammalian fuel utilisation during sustained exercise. *Comparative Biochemistry and Physiology B-Biochemistry & Molecular Biology*, 120, 89-107.

Brooks, G. A., Fahey, T. D. and Baldwin, K. M. (2005) *Exercise Physiology. Human Bioenergetics and Its Adaptations*. Boston; McGraw Hill.

Brooks, G. A. and Gaesser, G. A. (1980) End points of lactate and glucose metabolism after exhausting exercise. *Journal of Applied Physiology*, 49, 1057-1069.

Brooks, G. A. and Mercier, J. (1994) Balance of Carbohydrate and Lipid Utilisation During Exercise - the Crossover Concept. *Journal of Applied Physiology*, 76, 2253-2261.

Brooks, G. A., Stanley, W. C., Gertz, E. W., Wisneski, J. A., Morris, D. L. and Neese, R. A. (1985) Lactate Metabolism in Exercising Human Skeletal-Muscle - Evidence for Lactate Extraction During Net Lactate Release. *Federation Proceedings*, 44, 1013.

Brun, J. F., Jean, E., Ghanassia, E., Flavier, S. and Mercier, J. (2007) Metabolic training: new paradigms of exercise training for metabolic diseases with exercise calorimetry targeting individuals. *Annales de Readaptation et de Medicine Physique*..

Caputo, F. and Denadai, B. S. (2006) Exercise mode affects the time to achieve VO2max without influencing maximal exercise time at the intensity associated with VO2max in triathletes. *International Journal of Sports Medicine*, 27, 798-803.

Chavarren, J. and Calbet, J. A. L. (1999) Cycling efficiency and pedalling frequency in road cyclists. *European Journal of Applied Physiology and Occupational Physiology*, 80, 555-563.

Chudalla, R., Baerwalde, S., Schneider, G. and Maassen, N. (2006) Local and systemic effects on blood lactate concentration during exercise with small and large muscle groups. *Pflugers Archiv.European Journal of Physiology*, 452, 690-697.

Coggan, A. R., Kohrt, W. M., Spina, R. J., Kirwan, J. P., Bier, D. M. and Holloszy, J. O. (1992) Plasma glucose kinetics during exercise in subjects with high and low lactate thresholds. *Journal of Applied Physiology*, 73, 1873-1880.

Constantin-Teodosiu, D., Peirce, N. S., Fox, J. and Greenhaff, P. L. (2004) Muscle pyruvate availability can limit the flux, but not activation, of the pyruvate dehydrogenase complex during submaximal exercise in humans. *Journal of Physiology-London*, 561, 647-655.

Constantin-Teodosiu, D., Simpson, E. J. and Greenhaff, P. L. (1998) Effects of pyruvate, dichloroacetate and adrenaline infusion on pyruvate dehydrogenase complex activation and tricarboxylic acid cycle intermediates in human skeletal muscle. *Journal of Physiology-London*, 506P, 102P.

Constantin-Teodosiu, D., Simpson, E. J. and Greenhaff, P. L. (1999) The importance of pyruvate availability to PDC activation and anaplerosis in human skeletal muscle. *American Journal of Physiology-Endocrinology and Metabolism*, 276, E472-E478.

Coyle, E. F., Coggan, A. R., Hopper, M. K. and Walters, T. J. (1988) Determinants of Endurance in Well-Trained Cyclists. *Journal of Applied Physiology*, 64, 2622-2630.

Coyle, E. F., Jeukendrup, A. E., Wagenmakers, A. J. M. and Saris, W. H. M. (1997) Fatty acid oxidation is directly regulated by carbohydrate metabolism during exercise. *American Journal of Physiology-Endocrinology and Metabolism*, 36, E268-E275.

Denadai, B. S., Ruas, V. D. and Figueira, T. R. (2006) Maximal lactate steady state concentration independent of pedal cadence in active individuals. *European Journal of Applied Physiology and Occupational Physiology*, 96, 477-480.

Dennis, S. C. and Noakes, T. D. (1998) Physiological and metabolic responses to increasing work rates: Relevance for exercise prescription. *Journal of Sports Sciences*, 16, S77-S84.

Dennis, S. C., Noakes, T. D. and Bosch, A. N. (1992) Ventilation and blood lactate increase exponentially during incremental exercise. *Journal of Sports Sciences*, 10, 437-449.

Deschenes, M. R., Kraemer, W. J., Mccoy, R. W., Volek, J. S., Turner, B. M. and Weinlein, J. C. (2000) Muscle recruitment patterns regulate physiological responses during exercise of the same intensity. *American Journal of Physiology-Regulatory Integrative and Comparative Physiology*, 279, R2229-R2236.

Donovan, C. M. and Brooks, G. A. (1983) Endurance Training Affects Lactate Clearance, Not Lactate Production. *American Journal of Physiology*, 244, E83-E92.

Dore, E., Baker, J. S., Jammes, A., Graham, M., New, K. and Van Praagh, E. (2006) Upper body contribution during leg cycling peak power in teenage boys and girls. *Research in Sports Medicine*, 14, 245-257.

Ferguson, R. A., Ball, D., Krustrup, P., Aagaard, P., Kjaer, M., Sargeant, A. J., Hellsten, Y. and Bangsbo, J. (2001) Muscle oxygen uptake and energy turnover during dynamic exercise at different contraction frequencies in humans. *Journal of Physiology*, 536, 261-271.

Foss O, Hallen J (2004). The most economical cadence increases with increasing workload. *European Journal of Applied Physiology and Occupational Physiology*;92(4-5):443-51

Friedlander, A. L., Casazza, G. A., Horning, M. A., Usaj, A. and Brooks, G. A. (1999) Endurance training increases fatty acid turnover, but not fat oxidation, in young men. *Journal of Applied Physiology;* 86, 2097-2105.

Gaesser, G. A. and Brooks, G. A. (1975) Muscular efficiency during steady-rate exercise: effects of speed and work rate. *Journal of Applied Physiology*, 38, 1132-1139.

Gaesser, G. A. and Poole, D. C. (1996) The slow component of oxygen uptake kinetics in humans. *Exercise and Sport Science Reviews*, 24, 35-71.

Gladden, L. B. (2000) The role of skeletal muscle in lactate exchange during exercise: introduction. *Medicine and Science in Sports and Exercise*, 32, 753-755.

Gollnick, P. D., Piehl, K. and Saltin, B. (1974) Selective glycogen depletion pattern in human muscle fibres after exercise of varying intensity and at varying pedalling rates. *Journal of Physiology*, 241, 45-57.

Gonzalez-Haro, C., Galilea, P. A., Gonzalez-de-Suso, J. M., Drobnic, F. and Escanero, J. F. (2007) Maximal lipidic power in high competitive level triathletes and cyclists. *British Journal of Sports Medicine*, 41, 23-28.

Hagberg, J. M., Mullin, J. P., Giese, M. D. and Spitznagel, E. (1981) Effect of pedaling rate on submaximal exercise responses of competitive cyclists. *Journal of Applied Physiology*, 51, 447-451.

Hargreaves, M. (2004) Muscle glycogen and metabolic regulation. *Proc.Nutritional Society*, 63, 217-220.

Hargreaves, M. and Spriet, L. L. (2006) *Exercise Metabolism*. Human Kinetics, USA.

Henderson, G. C., Horning, M. A., Lehman, S. L., Wolfel, E. E., Bergman, B. C. and Brooks, G. A. (2004) Pyruvate shuttling during rest and exercise before and after endurance training in men. *Journal of Applied Physiology*, 97, 317-325.

Hill, A. V., Long, C. N. and Lupton, H. (1924) The effect of fatigue on the relation between work and speed, in contraction of human arm muscles. *Journal of Physiology*, 58, 334-337.

Howlett, R. A., Parolin, M. L., Dyck, D. J., Hultman, E., Jones, N. L., Heigenhauser, G. J. F. and Spriet, L. L. (1998) Regulation of skeletal muscle glycogen phosphorylase and PDH at varying exercise power outputs. *American Journal of Physiology-Regulatory Integrative and Comparative Physiology*, 44, R418-R425.

Howley, E. T., Bassett, D. R., Jr. and Welch, H. G. (1995) Criteria for maximal oxygen uptake: review and commentary. *Medicine and Science in Sports and Exercise*, 27, 1292-1301.

Hughes, E. F., Turner, S. C. and Brooks, G. A. (1982) Effects of glycogen depletion and pedaling speed on "anaerobic threshold". *Journal of Applied Physiology*, 52, 1598-1607.

Hughson, R. L., Weisiger, K. H. and Swanson, G. D. (1987) Blood Lactate Concentration Increases As A Continuous Function in Progressive Exercise. *Journal of Applied Physiology*, 62, 1975-1981.

Issekutz, B., Jr., Shaw, W. A. and Issekutz, T. B. (1975) Effect of lactate on FFA and glycerol turnover in resting and exercising dogs. *Journal of Applied Physiology*, 39, 349-353.

Jeukendrup, A. E. and Wallis, G. A. (2005) Measurement of substrate oxidation during exercise by means of gas exchange measurements. *International Journal of Sports Medicine*, 26, S28-S37.

Jones, A. M. and Poole, D. C. (2005) *Oxygen Uptake Kinetics in Sport , Exercise, and Medicine: Research and Practical Applications; Routledge; Great Brtitian.*

Jones, A. M., Wilkerson, D. P., Burnley, M. and Koppo, K. (2003) Prior heavy exercise enhances performance during subsequent perimaximal exercise. *Medicine and Science in Sports and Exercise*, 35, 2085-2092.

Kang, J., Hoffman, J. R., Wendell, M., Walker, H. and Hebert, M. (2004) Effect of contraction frequency on energy expenditure and substrate utilisation during upper and lower body exercise. *British Journal of Sports Medicine*, 38, 31-35.

Knechtle, B., Muller, G. and Knecht, H. (2004) Optimal exercise intensities for fat metabolism in handbike cycling and cycling. *Spinal Cord.*, 42, 564-572.

Lombardi, A. M., Fabris, R., Bassetto, F., Serra, R., Leturque, A., Federspil, G., Girard, J. and Vettor, R. (1999) Hyperlactatemia reduces muscle glucose uptake and GLUT-4 mRNA while increasing (E1 alpha)PDH gene expression in rat. *American Journal of Physiology-Endocrinology and Metabolism*, 276, E922-E929.

Mader, A. and Heck, H. (1986) A Theory of the Metabolic Origin of Anaerobic Threshold. *International Journal of Sports Medicine*, 7, 45-65.

Maeder, M., Wolber, T., Atefy, R., Gadza, M., Ammann, P., Myers, J. and Rickli, H. (2005) Impact of the exercise mode on exercise capacity: bicycle testing revisited. *Chest*, 128, 2804-2811.

Margaria, R., Edwards, H. T. and Dill, D. B. (1933) The possible mechanisms of contracting and paying the oxygen debt and the role of lactic acid in muscular contraction. *American Journal of Physiology*, 106, 689-715.

Matthews, J. I., Bush, B. A. and Morales, F. M. (1987) Microprocessor exercise physiology systems vs a nonautomated system. A comparison of data output. *Chest*, 92, 696-703.

McArdle, W. D., Katch, F. I. and Katch, V. L. (2001) *Exercise Physiology; Energy, Nutrition, and Human Performance*. Lippincott Wiliams & Wilkins, Philadelphia, Pennsylvania, USA.

McDaniel, J., Durstine, J. L., Hand, G. A. and Martin, J. C. (2002) Determinants of metabolic cost during submaximal cycling. *Journal of Applied Physiology*, 93, 823-828.

McDaniel, J., Subudhi, A. and Martin, J. C. (2005) Torso stabilization reduces the metabolic cost of producing cycling power. *Canadian Journal of Applied Physiology*, 30, 433-441.

Mcgarry, J. D., Mills, S. E., Long, C. S. and Foster, D. W. (1983) Observations on the Affinity for Carnitine, and Malonyl-Coa Sensitivity, of Carnitine Palmitoyltransferase-I in Animal and Human-Tissues - Demonstration of the Presence of Malonyl-Coa in Non-Hepatic Tissues of the Rat. *Biochemical Journal*, 214, 21-28.

Miller, B. F., Fattor, J. A., Jacobs, K. A., Horning, M. A., Navazio, F., Lindinger, M. I. and Brooks, G. A. (2002) Lactate and glucose interactions during rest and exercise in men: effect of exogenous lactate infusion. *Journal of Physiology-London*, 544, 963-975.

Motulsky, H. J. and Ransnas, L. A. (1987) Fitting Curves to Data Using Nonlinear-Regression - A Practical and Nonmathematical Review *FASEB Journal*, 1, 365-374.

Mourtzakis, M., Saltin, B., Graham, T. and Pilegaard, H. (2006) Carbohydrate metabolism during prolonged exercise and recovery: interactions between pyruvate dehydrogenase, fatty acids, and amino acids. *Journal of Applied Physiology*, 100, 1822-1830.

Murphy, E. J. (2006) Stable isotope methods for the in vivo measurement of lipogenesis and triglyceride metabolism. *J.Anim Sci.*, 84 Suppl, E94-104.

Myers, J., Walsh, D., Sullivan, M. and Froelicher, V. (1990) Effect of Sampling on Variability and Plateau in Oxygen-Uptake. *Journal of Applied Physiology*, 68, 404-410.

Nordby, P., Saltin, B. and Helge, J. W. (2006) Whole-body fat oxidation determined by graded exercise and indirect calorimetry: a role for muscle oxidative capacity? *Scandinavian Journal of Medicine & Science in Sports*, 16, 209-214.

Odland, L. M., Heigenhauser, G. J. F., Wong, D., Hollidge-Horvat, M. G. and Spriet, L. L. (1998) Effects of increased fat availability on fat-carbohydrate interaction during prolonged exercise in men. *American Journal of Physiology-Regulatory Integrative and Comparative Physiology*, 43, R894-R902.

Ozyener, F., Rossiter, H. B., Ward, S. A. and Whipp, B. J. (2001) Influence of exercise intensify on the on- and off-transient kinetics of pulmonary oxygen uptake in humans. *Journal of Physiology-London*, 533, 891-902.

Pagano, C., Granzotto, M., Sagrillo, E., Federspil, G. and Vettor, R. (1997) Effects of lactate infusion on hepatic and muscle glucose metabolism under hypoglycaemia. *Diabetologia*, 40, 925.

Pearce, F. J. and Connett, R. J. (1980) Effect of Lactate and Palmitate on Substrate Utilisation of Isolated Rat Soleus. *American Journal of Physiology*, 238, C149-C159.

Perez-Martin, A., Dumortier, M., Raynaud, E., Brun, J. F., Fedou, C., Bringer, J. and Mercier, J. (2001) Balance of substrate oxidation during submaximal exercise in lean and obese people. *Diabetes Metabolism*, 27, 466-474.

Peronnet, F. and Massicotte, D. (1991) Table of Nonprotein Respiratory Quotient - An Update. *Canadian Journal of Sport Sciences-Revue Canadienne des Sciences du Sport*, 16, 23-29.

Pringle, J. S. M., Doust, J. H., Carter, H., Tolfrey, K. and Jones, A. M. (2003) Effect of pedal rate on primary and slow-component oxygen uptake responses during heavy-cycle exercise. *Journal of Applied Physiology*, 94, 1501-1507.

Ranallo, R. F. and Rhodes, E. C. (1998) Lipid metabolism during exercise. *Sports Medicine*, 26, 29-42.

Robergs, R. A., Chwalbinskamoneta, J., Mitchell, J. B., Pascoe, D. D., Houmard, J. and Costill, D. L. (1990) Blood Lactate Threshold Differences Between Arterialized and Venous-Blood. *International Journal of Sports Medicine*, 11, 446-451.

Romijn, J. A., Coyle, E. F., Sidossis, L. S., Gastaldelli, A., Horowitz, J. F., Endert, E. and Wolfe, R. R. (1993) Regulation of endogenous fat and carbohydrate metabolism in relation to exercise intensity and duration. *American Journal of Physiology*, 265, E380-E391.

Rossiter, H. B., Kowalchuk, J. M. and Whipp, B. J. (2006) A test to establish maximum O2 uptake despite no plateau in the O2 uptake response to ramp incremental exercise. *Journal of Applied Physiology*, 100, 764-770.

Sargent, C., Scroop, G. C., Nemeth, P. M., Burnet, R. B. and Buckley, J. D. (2002) Maximal oxygen uptake and lactate metabolism are normal in chronic fatigue syndrome. *Medicine and Science in Sports and Exercise*, 34, 51-56.

Sawka, M. N. (1986) Physiology of upper body exercise. *Exercise and Sport Science Reviews*, 14, 175-211.

Sidossis, L. S., Gastaldelli, A., Klein, S. and Wolfe, R. R. (1997) Regulation of plasma fatty acid oxidation during low- and high-intensity exercise. *American Journal of Physiology-Endocrinology and Metabolism*, 35, E1065-E1070.

Spriet, L. L. (2002) Regulation of skeletal muscle fat oxidation during exercise in humans. *Medicine and Science in Sports and Exercise*, 34, 1477-1484.

Spriet, L. L. and Heigenhauser, G. J. F. (2002) Regulation of pyruvate dehydrogenase (PDH) activity in human skeletal muscle during exercise. *Exercise and Sport Sciences Reviews*, 30, 91-95.

Spriet, L. L., Howlett, R. A. and Heigenhauser, G. J. F. (2000) An enzymatic approach to lactate production in human skeletal muscle during exercise. *Medicine and Science in Sports and Exercise*, 32, 756-763.

Starritt, E. C., Howlett, R. A., Heigenhauser, G. J. F. and Spriet, L. L. (2000) Sensitivity of CPT I to malonyl-CoA in trained and untrained human skeletal muscle. *American Journal of Physiology-Endocrinology and Metabolism*, 278, E462-E468.

Stellingwerff, T., Watt, M. J., Heigenhauser, G. J. F. and Spriet, L. L. (2003) Effects of reduced free fatty acid availability on skeletal muscle PDH activation during aerobic exercise. *American Journal of Physiology-Endocrinology and Metabolism*, 284, E589-E596.

Stephens, B. R., Cole, A. S. and Mahon, A. D. (2006) The influence of biological maturation on fat and carbohydrate metabolism during exercise in males. *International Journal of Sport Nutrition and Exercise Metabolism*, 16, 166-179.

Stockhausen, W., Grathwohl, D., Burklin, C., Spranz, P. and Keul, J. (1997) Stage duration and increase of work load in incremental testing on a cycle ergometer. *European Journal of Applied Physiology and Occupational Physiology*, 76, 295-301.

Stringer, W., Wasserman, K. and Casaburi, R. (1995) The VCO2/VO2 relationship during heavy, constant work rate exercise reflects the rate of lactic acid accumulation. *European Journal of Applied Physiology and Occupational Physiology*, 72, 25-31.

Swain, D. P. and Wright, R. L. (1997) Prediction of VO2peak from submaximal cycle ergometry using 50 versus 80 rpm. *Medicine and Science in Sports and Exercise*, 29, 268-272.

Takaishi, T., Yasuda, Y., Ono, T. and Moritani, T. (1996) Optimal pedaling rate estimated from neuromuscular fatigue for cyclists. *Medicine and Science in Sports and Exercise*, 28, 1492-1497.

Trudeau, F., Bernier, S., De Glisezinski, I., Crampes, F., Dulac, F. and Riviere, D. (1999) Lack of antilipolytic effect of lactate in subcutaneous abdominal adipose tissue during exercise. *Journal of Applied Physiology*, 86, 1800-1804.

van Loon, L. J. C., Greenhaff, P. L., Teodosiu, D. C., Saris, W. H. M. and Wagenmakers, A. J. M. (2001) The effects of increasing exercise intensity on muscle fuel utilisation in humans. *Journal of Physiology-London*, 536, 295-304.

Venables, M. C., Achten, J. and Jeukendrup, A. E. (2005) Determinants of fat oxidation during exercise in healthy men and women: a cross-sectional study. *Journal of Applied Physiology*, 98, 160-167.

Vettor, R., Lombardi, A. M., Fabris, R., Pagano, C., Cusin, I., RohnerJeanrenaud, F., Federspil, G. and Jeanrenaud, B. (1997) Lactate infusion in anesthetized rats produces insulin resistance in heart and skeletal muscles. *Metabolism-Clinical and Experimental*, 46, 684-690.

von Duvillard, S. P. and Hagan, R. D. (1994) Independence of ventilation and blood lactate responses during graded exercise. *European Journal of Applied Physiology and Occupational Physiology*, 68, 298-302.

Wasserman, D. H., Lacy, D. B., Green, D. R., Williams, P. E. and Cherrington, A. D. (1987) Dynamics of Hepatic Lactate and Glucose Balances During Prolonged Exercise and Recovery in the Dog. *Journal of Applied Physiology*, 63, 2411-2417.

Wasserman, K. (2002) Exercise gas exchange, breath-by-breath. *American Journal of Respiratory and Critical Care Medicine*, 165, 325-326.

Wasserman, K., Beaver, W. L., Davis, J. A., Pu, J. Z., Heber, D. and Whipp, B. J. (1985) Lactate, Pyruvate, and Lactate-To-Pyruvate Ratio During Exercise and Recovery. *Journal of Applied Physiology*, 59, 935-940.

Wasserman, K., Beaver, W. L. and Whipp, B. J. (1990) Gas Exchange Theory and the Lactaic Acidosis (anaerobic) threshold. *Circulation*, 81, II-14-30.

Wasserman, K., Hansen, J. E., Sue, D. Y. and Whipp, B. J. (2005) *Principles of Exercise Testing and Interpretation*.

Wasserman. K, Whipp, B. J., Koyal, S. N. and Beaver, W. L. (1973) Anaerobic Threshold and Respiratory Gas-Exchange During Exercise. *Journal of Applied Physiology*, 35, 236-243.

Watt, M. J., Heigenhauser, G. J. F., LeBlanc, P. J., Inglis, J. G., Spriet, L. L. and Peters, S. J. (2004) Rapid upregulation of pyruvate dehydrogenase kinase activity in human skeletal muscle during prolonged exercise. *Journal of Applied Physiology*, 97, 1261-1267.

Whipp, B. J. (1994) The Slow Component of O-2 Uptake Kinetics During Heavy Exercise. *Medicine and Science in Sports and Exercise*, 26, 1319-1326.

Whipp, B. J. (2006) Physiological Mechanisms Dissociating Pulmonary CO2 and O2 Exchange Dynamics during Exercise. *Experimental Physiology*.

Whipp, B. J. and Ward, S. A. (1993) Pulmonary Gas-Exchange Kinetics During Exercise - Physiological Inferences of Model Order and Parameters. *Journal of Thermal Biology*, 18, 599-604.

Wieland OH. (1983) The mammalian pyruvate dehydrogenase complex: structure and regulation. *Reviews of Physiology, Biochemistry, and Pharmacology*, 96, 123-70.

Winder, W. W. (2001) Energy-sensing and signaling by AMP-activated protein kinase in skeletal muscle. *Journal of Applied Physiology*, 91, 1017-1028.

Woolford, S. M., Withers, R. T., Craig, N. P., Bourdon, P. C., Stanef, T. and McKenzie, I. (1999) Effect of pedal cadence on the accumulated oxygen deficit, maximal aerobic power and blood lactate transition thresholds of high-performance junior endurance cyclists. *European Journal of Applied Physiology and Occupational Physiology*, 80, 285-291.

Xu, F. and Rhodes, E. C. (1999) Oxygen uptake kinetics during exercise. *Sports Medicine*, 27, 313-327.

Yeh, M. P., Gardner, R. M., Adams, T. D., Yanowitz, F. G. and Crapo, R. O. (1983) Anaerobic Threshold - Problems of Determination and Validation. *Journal of Applied Physiology*, 55, 1178-1186.

Zoladz, J. A., Duda, K., Konturek, S. J., Sliwowski, Z., Pawlik, T. and Majerczak, J. (2002) Effect of different muscle shortening velocities during prolonged incremental cycling exercise on the plasma growth hormone, insulin, glucose, glucagon, cortisol, leptin and lactate concentrations. *Journal of Physiology and Pharmacology*, 53, 409-422.

Zoladz, J. A., Rademaker, A. C. and Sargeant, A. J. (2000) Human muscle power generating capability during cycling at different pedalling rates. *Experimental Physiology*, 85, 117-124.

CHAPTER TEN

APPENDICES

APPENDIX A

No	kel $(mmol.l^{-1})^2$	r-square	Residuals
1	1.003	0.86	457.80
2	1.406	0.97	144.18
3	.835	0.83	1428.83
4	1.356	0.69	834.55
5	1.210	0.94	239.66
6	1.361	0.77	303.61
7	1.440	0.96	259.99
8	1.622	0.84	800.82
9	1.232	0.82	745.07
10	.537	0.77	440.83
11	2.136	0.91	366.02
12	3.839	0.97	115.93
13	1.979	0.94	177.37
14	2.128	0.85	720.49
15	2.298	0.91	346.30
16	1.042	0.91	223.45
17	2.218	0.77	1219.82
18	2.213	0.65	2671.86
19	4.403	0.83	883.06
20	1.160	0.83	1133.31
21	2.706	0.93	386.67
Mean	1.815	0.855	661.89
Std. Deviation	0.952	0.089	595.18
Minimum	0.537	0.650	
Maximum	4.403	0.970	

Table A1. Individual kel data describing the BLC-RPY interrelationship

APPENDIX B

no	kel 120s	r²	kel 60s	r²	kel 30s	r²
1	1.625	0.946	1.159	0.924	1.003	0.860
2	1.803	0.962	1.492	0.948	1.406	0.965
3	1.096	0.853	0.943	0.824	0.835	0.829
4	1.640	0.677	1.552	0.653	1.356	0.692
5	1.634	0.937	1.521	0.913	1.210	0.941
6	2.211	0.955	1.489	0.888	1.361	0.773
7	2.063	0.973	1.674	0.963	1.440	0.958
8	1.759	0.841	1.621	0.838	1.622	0.844
9	1.764	0.819	1.433	0.784	1.232	0.816
10	0.817	0.932	0.671	0.878	0.537	0.769
11	3.324	0.910	2.761	0.902	2.136	0.909
12	6.594	0.953	4.963	0.962	3.839	0.972
13	2.869	0.945	2.575	0.946	1.979	0.939
14	2.795	0.922	2.593	0.846	2.128	0.853
15	3.893	0.901	3.218	0.890	2.298	0.910
16	1.533	0.894	1.340	0.873	1.042	0.912
17	2.921	0.914	2.803	0.797	2.218	0.765
18	2.349	0.792	2.424	0.668	2.213	0.651
19	5.159	0.799	5.169	0.789	4.403	0.830
20	1.620	0.851	1.430	0.816	1.160	0.831
21	4.421	0.946	3.799	0.944	2.706	0.932
Mean	2.566*	0.892*	2.220**	0.859	1.815	0.855
SD	1.433	0.074	1.234	0.087	0.952	0.089

Table B1. Individual kel values at averages of 120, 60 and 30s

Intensity (%)	$\dot{V}O_2$ (ml.min^{-1}) (Mean ± SD)		
	120s	60s	30s
25	1169 ± 128*	1311 ± 128	1310 ± 137
30	1343 ± 151*	1483 ± 151	1484 ± 157
35	1518 ± 175*	1655 ± 176	1658 ± 180
40	1693 ± 199*	1827 ± 202	1832 ± 206
45	1868 ± 225*	1999 ± 229	2006 ± 232
50	2043 ± 251*	2170 ± 256	2180 ± 259
55	2218 ± 277*	2342 ± 283	2354 ± 287
60	2393 ± 304*	2514 ± 311**	2528 ± 315
65	2567 ± 331*	2686 ± 339**	2702 ± 344
70	2742 ± 358*	2858 ± 367**	2876 ± 372
75	2917 ± 385*	3030 ± 395**	3051 ± 401
80	3092 ± 412*	3201 ± 424**	3225 ± 431
85	3267 ± 439*	3373 ± 452**	3399 ± 460
90	3442 ± 466*	3545 ± 481**	3573 ± 489
95	3617 ± 494*	3717 ± 509**	3747 ± 519

Table B2. Averaging effects on $\dot{V}O_2$ at given exercise intensities. *Significantly lower $\dot{V}O_2$ in 120s than 60 and 30s. **Significantly lower $\dot{V}O_2$ in 60 than 30s

Intensity (%)	$\dot{V}CO_2$ (ml.min^{-1}) (Mean ± SD)		
	120s	60s	30s
25	933 ± 109*	1053 ± 112	1075 ± 124
30	1078 ± 125*	1199 ± 125	1223 ± 131
35	1232 ± 144*	1353 ± 144**	1380 ± 147
40	1394 ± 167*	1517 ± 167**	1545 ± 169
45	1565 ± 191*	1691 ± 192**	1721 ± 195
50	1747 ± 216*	1875 ± 219**	1908 ± 223
55	1939 ± 242*	2070 ± 246**	2105 ± 252
60	2142 ± 269*	2278 ± 275**	2315 ± 281
65	2357 ± 296*	2498 ± 304**	2538 ± 311
70	2585 ± 325*	2732 ± 333**	2776 ± 341
75	2826 ± 355*	2980 ± 364**	3028 ± 372

80	3082 ± 386*	3245 ± 396**	3297 ± 404
85	3352 ± 420*	3526 ± 430**	3583 ± 438
90	3640 ± 456*	3825 ± 466**	3888 ± 475
95	3944 ± 496*	4144 ± 507**	4213 ± 518

Table B3. Averaging effects on $\dot{V}CO_2$ at given exercise intensities. *Significantly lower in 120s than 60 and 30s. **Significantly lower in 60 than 30s

Intensity (%)	RQ (Mean ± SD)		
	120s	60s	30s
25	0.80 ± 0.05	0.80 ± 0.06**	0.82 ± 0.07
30	0.80 ± 0.04	0.81 ± 0.05**	0.83 ± 0.05
35	0.81 ± 0.04*	0.82 ± 0.04**	0.83 ± 0.04
40	0.82 ± 0.04*	0.83 ± 0.04**	0.84 ± 0.04
45	0.84 ± 0.04*	0.85 ± 0.04**	0.86 ± 0.04
50	0.86 ± 0.04*	0.86 ± 0.04**	0.88 ± 0.04
55	0.87 ± 0.04*	0.88 ± 0.04**	0.90 ± 0.04
60	0.90 ± 0.04*	0.91 ± 0.04**	0.92 ± 0.04
65	0.92 ± 0.04*	0.93 ± 0.04**	0.94 ± 0.04
70	0.94 ± 0.04*	0.96 ± 0.05**	0.97 ± 0.04
75	0.97 ± 0.04*	0.99 ± 0.05**	0.99 ± 0.04
80	1.00 ± 0.05*	1.02 ± 0.05**	1.02 ± 0.05
85	1.03 ± 0.05*	1.05 ± 0.05**	1.06 ± 0.05

Table B4. Averaging effects on RQ at given exercise intensities. *Significantly lower in 120s than 60 and 30s. **Significantly lower in 60 than 30s.

Intensity	Relative rate of CHO oxidation (%)		
(%)	(Mean ± SD)		
	120s	60s	30s
25	32.13 ± 16.39	34.02 ± 21.00**	40.26 ± 24.69
30	33.47 ± 13.28**	35.71 ± 16.87**	41.22 ± 18.41
35	36.36 ± 12.13**	38.83 ± 14.78**	43.77 ± 14.89
40	40.43 ± 12.05*	43.09 ± 14.03**	47.56 ± 13.44
45	45.43 ± 12.41*	48.30 ± 13.99**	52.39 ± 13.26
50	51.23 ± 12.89*	54.34 ± 14.24**	58.11 ± 13.62
55	57.74 ± 13.32*	61.13 ± 14.54**	64.64 ± 14.07
60	64.89 ± 13.70*	68.62 ± 14.78**	71.65 ± 13.78
65	72.66 ± 14.03*	76.30 ± 14.05**	78.96 ± 12.72
70	80.51 ± 13.61*	84.08 ± 12.84**	86.38 ± 11.14
75	87.91 ± 12.26*	91.50 ± 11.40	93.33 ± 9.54
80	94.04 ± 10.55*	96.01 ± 9.03	96.98 ± 7.10
85	96.68 ± 8.26	97.56 ± 6.39	98.22 ± 4.53

Table B5. Effects of averaging on RPY at given exercise intensities. *Significantly lower than 60 and 30s. **Significantly lower than 30s.

Intensity	Relative rate of Fat oxidation (%)		
(%)	(Mean ± SD)		
	120s	60s	30s
25	67.87 ± 16.39	65.98 ± 21.00**	59.74 ± 24.69
30	66.53 ± 13.28**	64.29 ± 16.87**	58.78 ± 18.41
35	63.64 ± 12.13**	61.17 ± 14.78**	56.23 ± 14.89
40	59.57 ± 12.05*	56.91 ± 14.03**	52.44 ± 13.44
45	54.57 ± 12.41*	51.70 ± 13.99**	47.61 ± 13.26
50	48.77 ± 12.89*	45.66 ± 14.24**	41.89 ± 13.62
55	42.26 ± 13.32*	38.87 ± 14.54**	35.36 ± 14.07
60	35.11 ± 13.70*	31.38 ± 14.78**	28.35 ± 13.78
65	27.34 ± 14.03*	23.70 ± 14.05**	21.04 ± 12.72
70	19.49 ± 13.61*	15.92 ± 12.84**	13.62 ± 11.14
75	12.09 ± 12.26*	8.50 ± 11.40	6.6 7 ±9.54
80	5.96 ± 10.55*	3.99 ± 9.03	3.02 ± 7.10
85	3.22 ± 8.26	2.44 ± 6.39	1.78 ± 4.53

Table B6. Effects of averaging on relative fat oxidation rates at given exercise intensities. *Significantly higher than 60 and 30s. **Significantly higher than 30s.

Intensity (%)	CHO Oxidation g.min^{-1} (Mean ± SD)		
	120s	60s	30s
25	0.56 ± 0.33*	0.63 ± 0.37	0.63 ± 0.37
30	0.67 ± 0.28*	0.73 ± 0.31	0.73 ± 0.31
35	0.80 ± 0.27*	0.87 ± 0.28	0.87 ± 0.29
40	0.97 ± 0.28*	1.04 ± 0.29	1.05 ± 0.29
45	1.18 ± 0.31*	1.26 ± 0.32	1.26 ± 0.32
50	1.43 ± 0.35*	1.52 ± 0.36	1.52 ± 0.36
55	1.73 ± 0.40*	1.82 ± 0.41	1.83 ± 0.41
60	2.06 ± 0.43*	2.17 ± 0.43	2.18 ± 0.44
65	2.44 ± 0.44*	2.55 ± 0.44	2.56 ± 0.44
70	2.85 ± 0.44*	2.97 ± 0.45	2.99 ± 0.45
75	3.28 ± 0.47*	3.40 ± 0.48	3.43 ± 0.48
80	3.62 ± 0.53*	3.74 ± 0.54	3.77 ± 0.54
85	3.87 ± 0.54*	4.00 ± 0.55	4.03 ± 0.56

Table B7. Effects of averaging on CHO oxidation rates at given exercise intensities. *Significantly lower than 60 and 30s. **Significantly lower than 30s.

Intensity (%)	Fat Oxidation g.min^{-1} (Mean ± SD)		
	120s	60s	30s
25	0.40± 0.11	0.43 ± 0.15**	0.39 ± 0.17
30	0.45 ± 0.11	0.48 ± 0.14**	0.44 ± 0.15
35	0.48 ± 0.11	0.51 ± 0.14**	0.47 ± 0.15
40	0.50 ± 0.12	0.52 ± 0.15**	0.48 ± 0.15
45	0.51 ± 0.14**	0.52 ± 0.16**	0.48 ± 0.16
50	0.50 ± 0.16**	0.50 ± 0.18**	0.46 ± 0.17
55	0.47 ± 0.17**	0.46 ± 0.19**	0.42 ± 0.18
60	0.42 ± 0.19**	0.40 ± 0.21**	0.36 ± 0.19
65	0.35 ± 0.20**	0.32 ± 0.21**	0.29 ± 0.19
70	0.27 ± 0.20**	0.23 ± 0.20**	0.20 ± 0.17
75	0.18 ± 0.19**	0.13 ± 0.19**	0.11 ± 0.15

Intensity (%)			
80	0.10 ± 0.17**	0.07 ± 0.15	0.05 ± 0.12
85	0.05 ± 0.14**	0.04 ± 0.11	0.03 ± 0.08

Table B8. Effects of averaging on fat oxidation rates at given exercise intensities. *Significantly higher than 60 and 30s. **Significantly higher than 30s.

Intensity (%)	CHO (120s) Kcal.min^{-1}	CHO (60-s) Kcal.min^{-1}	CHO (30-s) Kcal.min^{-1}
25	2.26 ± 1.30*	2.51 ± 1.48	2.51 ± 1.47
30	2.66 ± 1.13*	2.92 ± 1.25	2.92 ± 1.25
35	3.20 ± 1.06*	3.47 ± 1.14	3.48 ± 1.14
40	3.88 ± 1.11*	4.17 ± 1.15	4.18 ± 1.16
45	4.71 ± 1.24*	5.03 ± 1.27	5.05 ± 1.28
50	5.72 ± 1.41*	6.06 ± 1.44	6.09 ± 1.45
55	6.90 ± 1.60*	7.28 ± 1.63	7.32 ± 1.64
60	8.25 ± 1.71*	8.66 ± 1.74**	8.71 ± 1.74
65	9.75 ± 1.75*	10.20 ± 1.78**	10.26 ± 1.78
70	11.40 ± 1.78*	11.87 ± 1.79**	11.94 ± 1.79
75	13.11 ± 1.90*	13.61 ± 1.91**	13.70 ± 1.91
80	14.47 ± 2.13*	14.98 ± 2.16**	15.09 ± 2.17
85	15.49 ± 2.17*	15.99 ± 2.21**	16.11 ± 2.23

Table B9. Effects of averaging on energy expenditure from CHO at given exercise intensities. *Significantly lower than 60 and 30s. **Significantly lower than 30s.

Intensity (%)	Fat (120s) Kcal.min^{-1}	Fat (60-s) Kcal.min^{-1}	Fat (30-s) Kcal.min^{-1}
25	3.56 ± 0.97	3.90 ± 1.36**	3.54 ± 1.56
30	4.01 ± 0.95	4.29 ± 1.28**	3.94 ± 1.38
35	4.33 ± 1.01	4.56 ± 1.29**	4.20 ± 1.31
40	4.52 ± 1.12	4.68 ± 1.36**	4.33 ± 1.32
45	4.57 ± 1.26**	4.65 ± 1.47**	4.30 ± 1.41
50	4.48 ± 1.40**	4.47 ± 1.60**	4.12 ± 1.53
55	4.22 ± 1.54**	4.11 ± 1.73**	3.76 ± 1.66
60	3.79 ± 1.67**	3.57 ± 1.85**	3.25 ± 1.71
65	3.18 ± 1.80*	2.90 ± 1.87**	2.59 ± 1.67
70	2.44 ± 1.83*	2.10 ± 1.80**	1.80 ± 1.54
75	1.63 ± 1.74*	1.21 ± 1.67	0.96 ± 1.37

| 80 | 0.87 ± 1.57* | 0.60 ± 1.39 | 0.45 ± 1.06 |
| 85 | 0.49 ± 1.29 | 0.39 ± 1.03 | 0.28 ± 0.71 |

Table B10. Effects of averaging on energy expenditure from fat at given exercise intensities. *Significantly higher than 60 and 30s. **Significantly higher than 30s.

| | $\dot{V}O_2 = a + b*intensity$ | | | | | |
| No | a | | | b | | |
	120s	60s	30s	120s	60s	30s
1	349.18	457.56	494.75	35.25	34.68	34.16
2	137.42	355.74	308.76	40.70	39.21	39.98
3	277.67	381.59	380.52	50.13	50.33	50.57
4	373.08	474.61	461.05	28.59	28.15	28.47
5	440.89	555.26	644.48	35.95	35.94	35.13
6	412.19	573.79	485.08	27.29	26.54	28.32
7	272.53	346.40	215.90	31.33	31.62	33.20
8	348.60	366.48	365.34	38.20	39.24	39.87
9	309.50	423.78	413.74	32.30	32.08	32.64
10	438.22	599.16	531.06	29.31	28.59	29.77
11	87.32	268.53	281.67	39.32	38.57	39.03
12	178.25	406.89	245.16	44.21	43.46	46.61
13	294.02	478.82	476.16	36.67	35.41	35.54
14	276.15	353.74	354.17	30.59	31.00	30.97
15	396.94	557.95	563.78	34.81	35.26	35.42
16	273.54	453.56	429.05	33.46	32.17	32.54
17	213.16	628.78	680.47	30.28	26.28	26.28
18	269.76	445.19	422.76	36.83	36.30	36.48
19	238.58	448.31	386.46	36.58	35.57	36.81
20	319.29	534.47	625.08	33.19	31.82	30.91
21	275.25	381.34	456.05	29.38	29.51	28.50
Mean	294.36	452.00	439.12	34.97	34.37	34.82
SD	92.94	95.28	125.59	5.56	5.79	6.04

Table B11. Parameters of $\dot{V}O_2$ fittings using a linear regression model.

148

	$\dot{V}CO_2 = ae^{b*intensity} + c$								
	a			b			c		
No	120s	60s	30	120s	60s	30	120s	60s	30
1	3724.85	7344.87	7371.40	0.008	0.005	0.005	-3526.083	-7198.160	-7184.273
2	1820.34	2366.50	2984.77	0.013	0.011	0.009	-1537.503	-1999.094	-2709.146
3	2353.36	2376.20	2534.67	0.012	0.012	0.012	-2010.769	-1963.956	-2134.852
4	1155.84	1256.74	1060.24	0.012	0.012	0.013	-640.150	-684.711	-431.676
5	3335.74	2566.34	1494.52	0.008	0.010	0.013	-3036.087	-2124.850	-802.108
6	1012.85	551.07	420.88	0.014	0.019	0.023	-513.077	240.573	391.123
7	1895.80	2542.99	2530.79	0.011	0.009	0.010	-1714.655	-2397.778	-2447.865
8	1646.46	1692.53	1700.04	0.013	0.013	0.013	-3526.08	-7198.16	-7184.27
9	3911.01	3955.19	5414.04	0.007	0.007	0.006	-1537.50	-1999.09	-2709.15
10	1483.57	1569.89	2398.36	0.012	0.012	0.009	-2010.77	-1963.96	-2134.85
11	1923.47	1234.64	772.94	0.012	0.015	0.019	-640.15	-684.71	-431.68
12	1733.22	1696.70	3346.03	0.013	0.013	0.009	-3036.09	-2124.85	-802.11
13	5196.76	3465.29	4015.59	0.006	0.008	0.007	-513.08	240.57	391.12
14	630.46	847.00	977.28	0.019	0.017	0.016	-1714.65	-2397.78	-2447.87
15	5377.02	3517.40	4109.55	0.005	0.007	0.007	-1190.26	-1209.92	-1221.48
16	932.07	495.85	336.25	0.017	0.022	0.025	-3797.35	-3743.21	-5264.73
17	1128.61	1411.03	1945.84	0.014	0.013	0.011	-995.43	-962.05	-1925.02
18	1827.40	2551.01	2167.88	0.012	0.010	0.011	-1711.30	-757.54	-86.97
19	2446.86	1897.44	1396.87	0.010	0.011	0.014	-1374.92	-1187.93	-3143.56
20	2548.75	1877.03	1665.04	0.010	0.012	0.012	-5005.91	-3050.45	-3602.32
21	936.04	690.82	868.43	0.015	0.018	0.016	-126.77	-370.45	-518.56
Mean	2239.07	2186.02	2357.69	0.011	0.012	0.012	-5207.16	-3178.37	-3767.79
SD	1352.71	1526.36	1741.71	0.003	0.004	0.005	-437.95	301.24	585.06

Table B12. Parameters of $\dot{V}CO_2$ fittings using a 3-parameter mono-exponential model

Intensity	Difference in $\dot{V}O_2$ (%) Mean ± SD			Difference in $\dot{V}CO_2$ (%) Mean ± SD		
	60-120s	30-120s	30-60s	60-120s	30-120s	30-60s
25	12 ± 6	12 ± 7	0 ± 4	13 ± 6	16 ± 10	2 ± 6
30	11 ± 5	11 ± 6	0 ± 3	11 ± 4	14 ± 7	2 ± 4
35	9 ± 4	9 ± 5	0 ± 2	10 ± 3	12 ± 5	2 ± 3
40	8 ± 3	8 ± 4	0 ± 2	9 ± 3	11 ± 4	2 ± 3
45	7 ± 2	7 ± 3	0 ± 2	8 ± 2	10 ± 4	2 ± 2
50	6 ± 2	7 ± 3	0 ± 1	7 ± 2	9 ± 3	2 ± 2
55	6 ± 2	6 ± 2	1 ± 1	7 ± 2	9 ± 3	2 ± 2
60	5 ± 1	6 ± 2	1 ± 1	6 ± 2	8 ± 3	2 ± 2
65	5 ± 1	5 ± 2	1 ± 1	6 ± 2	8 ± 3	2 ± 2
70	4 ± 1	5 ± 1	1 ± 1	6 ± 2	7 ± 3	2 ± 2
75	4 ± 1	5 ± 1	1 ± 1	6 ± 1	7 ± 3	2 ± 2
80	4 ± 1	4 ± 1	1 ± 1	5 ± 1	7 ± 2	2 ± 1
85	3 ± 1	4 ± 1	1 ± 1	5 ± 1	7 ± 2	2 ± 1
90	3 ± 1	4± 1	1 ± 1	5 ± 1	7 ± 3	2 ± 2
95	3 ± 1	4±1	1 ± 1	5 ± 2	7 ± 3	2 ± 2
Mean	5.98	6.49	0.50	7.37	9.28	1.91
SD	2.94	2.65	0.29	2.50	2.76	0.26

Table B13. Relative averaging induced differences for $\dot{V}O_2$ and $\dot{V}CO_2$ at given exercise intensities.

No	Difference in Peak $\dot{V}O_2$ (%)			Difference in Peak $\dot{V}CO_2$ (%)		
	60-120s	30-120s	30-60s	60-120s	30-120s	30-60s
1	-.16	-.03	.14	1.78	2.41	.63
2	.38	.38	.00	.92	-.02	-.95
3	1.86	1.50	-.36	4.63	5.43	.81
4	1.15	1.49	.33	2.21	2.18	-.03
5	3.53	4.74	1.20	5.18	7.44	2.26
6	3.71	6.68	2.96	6.16	11.70	5.54
7	2.32	3.08	.76	4.88	6.24	1.37
8	2.78	3.84	1.05	3.96	6.03	2.07
9	2.65	2.88	.23	4.35	5.51	1.16
10	2.23	3.32	1.09	3.38	4.39	1.01

11	3.11	5.42	2.31	7.52	12.71	5.19
12	3.68	4.66	.98	5.43	8.34	2.91
13	1.77	1.61	-.16	3.16	4.04	.87
14	2.47	2.38	-.09	5.12	4.92	-.20
15	6.48	7.37	.89	9.04	11.72	2.67
16	4.28	4.80	.52	6.30	7.53	1.23
17	2.74	4.64	1.91	5.00	7.88	2.88
18	3.04	3.39	.35	4.66	6.74	2.08
19	5.03	7.01	1.99	6.97	10.42	3.45
20	3.26	4.19	.93	5.19	6.31	1.12
21	5.28	4.71	-.57	6.29	6.42	.13
Mean	2.93	3.72	.78	4.86	6.59	1.72
SD	1.56	2.04	.92	1.92	3.23	1.65

Table B14. Relative averaging induced differences for peak $\dot{V}O_2$ and $\dot{V}CO_2$.

APPENDIX C

Subject No.	kel for 2-min (mmol.l^{-1})^2	r^2	kel for 6-min (mmol.l^{-1})^2	r^2
1	1.17	1.00	1.59	0.99
2	1.45	0.86	0.98	0.99
3	1.55	0.94	0.72	0.97
4	0.70	0.74	1.29	0.71
5	1.24	0.95	1.45	0.89
6	1.25	0.83	0.57	0.55
7	1.14	0.91	0.53	0.94
8	1.35	0.81	0.48	0.83
9	0.85	0.74	3.26	0.91
10	0.48	0.89	1.09	0.77
11	2.48	0.49	0.85	0.79
Mean ± SD	1.241 ± 0.523	0.82 ± 0.13	1.164 ± 0.788	0.84 ± 0.13

Table C1. Individual kel values at 2 vs. 6 min protocols.

Intensity (%)	RPY 2-min Mean ± SD	RPY 6-min Mean ± SD	RFAT 2-min Mean ± SD	RFAT 6-min Mean ± SD
25	49.12 ± 15.02	49.17 ± 12.14	50.88 ± 15.02	50.83 ± 12.14
30	52.96 ± 15.12	51.66 ± 12.56	47.04 ± 15.12	48.34 ± 12.56
40	57.15 ± 14.99	54.50 ± 13.10	42.85 ± 14.99	45.50 ± 13.10
45	61.64 ± 14.56	57.73 ± 13.63	38.36 ± 14.56	42.27 ± 13.63
50	66.35 ± 13.84	61.35 ± 13.99	33.65 ± 13.84	38.65 ± 13.99
55	71.15 ± 12.87	65.37 ± 14.06	28.85 ± 12.87	34.63 ± 14.06

60	75.87 ± 11.76	69.75 ± 13.78	24.13 ± 11.76	30.25 ± 13.78
65	80.33 ± 10.58	74.39 ± 13.10	19.67 ± 10.58	25.61 ± 13.10
70	84.41 ± 9.36	79.11 ± 12.02	15.59 ± 9.36	20.89 ± 12.02
75	87.98 ± 8.05	83.69 ± 10.51	12.02 ± 8.05	16.31 ± 10.51
80	91.01 ± 6.62	87.88 ± 8.63	8.99 ± 6.62	12.12 ± 8.63
85	93.50 ± 5.07	91.49 ± 6.50	6.50 ± 5.07	8.51 ± 6.50
90	95.47 ± 3.57	94.37 ± 4.42	4.53 ± 3.57	5.63 ± 4.42
95	96.95 ± 2.29	96.47 ± 2.70	3.05 ± 2.29	3.53 ± 2.70

Table C2. RPY, and RFAT data at given exercise intensities at 2 vs. 6-min protocols.

No.	kel 2nd min (mmol.l⁻¹)²	r^2	kel 4th min (mmol.l⁻¹)²	r^2	kel 6th min (mmol.l⁻¹)²	r^2
1	1.267	0.836	2.101	0.878	1.594	0.994
2	1.555	0.870	0.836	0.778	0.983	0.989
3	0.743	0.926	0.747	0.945	0.723	0.967
4	1.860	0.494	1.764	0.678	1.287	0.708
5	1.849	0.928	1.495	0.821	1.446	0.892
6	0.865	0.605	0.727	0.671	0.573	0.548
7	1.283	0.702	0.619	0.836	0.530	0.940
8	0.614	0.562	0.478	0.691	0.478	0.832
9	5.000	0.929	2.970	0.730	3.256	0.914
10	0.952	0.961	0.715	0.931	1.092	0.772
11	1.155	0.812	0.938	0.704	0.846	0.785
Mean ± SD	1.558 ± 1.214	0.784 ± 0.166	1.217 ± 0.779	0.788 ± 0.101	1.164 ± 0.788	0.84 ± 0.13

Table C3. Individual kel values at the 2nd, 4th, and 6th min of a 6 min protocols.

APPENDIX D

Subject No.	kel (mmol.l^{-1})^2 50 rpm	r^2	kel (mmol.l^{-1})^2 100rpm	r^2
1	2.136	0.909	1.181	0.928
2	3.839	0.972	2.322	0.923
3	1.979	0.939	2.779	0.938
4	2.128	0.853	2.415	0.937
5	2.298	0.91	2.014	0.968
6	1.042	0.912	1.662	0.85
7	2.213	0.651	3.936	0.886
8	4.403	0.83	4.996	0.904
9	1.16	0.831	1.446	0.867
10	2.706	0.932	2.397	0.822
11	0.835	0.829	1.44	0.889
Mean ± SD	2.25 ± 1.10	0.87 ± 0.09	2.42 ± 1.15	0.90 ± 0.04

Table D1. Individual levels of kel at 50 and 100 rpm.

Intensity (%)	$\dot{V}O_2$ ml.min^{-1} 50 rpm	$\dot{V}O_2$ ml.min^{-1} 100 rpm	$\dot{V}CO_2$ ml.min^{-1} 50 rpm	$\dot{V}CO_2$ ml.min^{-1} 100 rpm
30	1520 ± 170*	2012 ± 317	1246 ± 119**	1759 ± 300
35	1704 ± 199*	2171 ± 327	1403 ± 143**	1913 ± 283
40	1887 ± 229*	2329 ± 340	1569 ± 172**	2073 ± 274
45	2070 ± 260*	2487 ± 356	1747 ± 203**	2241 ± 274
50	2254 ± 291*	2646 ± 373	1936 ± 236**	2417 ± 281

55	2437 ± 323*	2804 ± 393	2138 ± 269**	2602 ± 295
60	2620 ± 356*	2962 ± 414	2354 ± 302**	2796 ± 314
65	2804 ± 388*	3120 ± 437	2584 ± 335**	3000 ± 338
70	2987 ± 421*	3279 ± 461	2831 ± 368**	3216 ± 365
75	3170 ± 453*	3437 ± 487	3094 ± 402**	3444 ± 396
80	3354 ± 486*	3595 ± 513	3376 ± 436**	3685 ± 430
85	3537 ± 519*	3754 ± 539	3678 ± 471**	3942 ± 471
90	3720 ± 552*	3912 ± 567	4001 ± 510**	4214 ± 520
95	3904 ± 585*	4070 ± 595	4348 ± 553**	4506 ± 583

Table D2. $\dot{V}O_2$ and $\dot{V}CO_2$ data for given exercise intensities at 50 vs. 100 rpm. *Significantly lower $\dot{V}O_2$ than 100 rpm. **Significantly lower $\dot{V}CO_2$ than 50 rpm.

Intensity (%)	BLC at 50 rpm (mmol.l⁻¹)	BLC at 100 rpm (mmol.l⁻¹)
30	1.2 ± 0.4*	1.8 ± 0.4
35	1.3 ± 0.4*	2.0 ± 0.4
40	1.4 ± 0.4*	2.2 ± 0.5
45	1.6 ± 0.4*	2.4 ± 0.6
50	1.8 ± 0.4*	2.7 ± 0.6
55	2.0 ± 0.5*	3.0 ± 0.7
60	2.3 ± 0.6*	3.4 ± 0.8
65	2.6 ± 0.6*	3.9 ± 0.9
70	3.0 ± 0.7*	4.4 ± 1.0
75	3.4 ± 0.8*	5.1 ± 1.1
80	4.0 ± 0.9*	5.9 ± 1.2

85	4.7 ± 1.0*	6.8 ± 1.2
90	5.6 ± 1.2*	8.0 ± 1.3
95	6.7 ± 1.4*	9.4 ± 1.4

Table D3. BLC levels for given exercise intensities at 50 vs. 100 rpm. *Significantly lower than 100 rpm

Intensity (%)	RPY (%)	RPY (%)	RFAT (%)	RFAT (%)
	50 rpm	**100 rpm**	**50 rpm**	**100 rpm**
30	40.8 ± 13.2	57.6 ± 11.6*	59.2 ± 13.2**	42.4 ±11.6
35	44.6 ± 12.4	61.7 ± 11.21*	55.4 ± 12.4**	38.3 ± 11.1
40	49.0 ± 11.6	65.9 ± 10.7*	51.0 ± 11.6**	34.1 ± 10.7
45	53.8 ± 11.0	70.1 ± 10.2*	46.2 ± 11.0**	29.9 ± 10.2
50	58.9 ±10.4	74.2 ± 9.6*	41.1 ± 10.4**	25.7 ± 9.6
55	64.2 ± 9.8	78.2 ± 8.8*	35.8 ± 9.8**	21.8 ± 8.8
60	69.5 ± 9.2	82.0 ± 7.7*	30.5 ± 9.2**	18.1 ± 7.7
65	74.6 ± 8.3	85.4 ± 6.4*	25.4 ± 8.3**	14.6 ± 6.4
70	79.5 ± 7.2	88.5 ± 5.1*	20.5 ± 7.2**	11.5 ± 5.1
75	83.8 ± 6.0	91.1 ± 3.8*	16.2 ± 6.0**	8.9 ± 3.8
80	87.5 ± 5.0	93.3 ± 2.8*	12.5 ± 5.0**	6.7 ± 2.8

Table D4. RPY and RFAT for given exercise intensities at 50 vs. 100 rpm. *Significantly lower RPY than 100 rpm. **Significantly lower RFAT than 100 rpm.

Intensity (%)	CHO oxidation g.min^{-1}	CHO oxidation g.min^{-1}	Fat oxidation g.min^{-1}	Fat oxidation g.min^{-1}
	50 rpm	**100 rpm**	**50 rpm**	**100 rpm**
30	0.72 ± 0.28*	1.40 ± 0.53	0.46 ± 0.16	0.42 ± 0.21
35	0.83 ± 0.23*	1.57 ± 0.42	0.51 ± 0.15	0.43 ± 0.19

40	0.98 ± 0.21*	1.77 ± 0.34	0.53 ± 0.14**	0.43 ± 0.19
45	1.18 ± 0.23*	2.00 ± 0.31	0.54 ± 0.14**	0.41 ± 0.20
50	1.43 ± 0.26*	2.26 ± 0.31	0.53 ± 0.15**	0.38 ± 0.21
55	1.73 ± 0.30*	2.56 ± 0.33	0.50 ± 0.15**	0.34 ± 0.23
60	2.08 ± 0.35*	2.89 ± 0.36	0.45 ± 0.16**	0.28 ± 0.24
65	2.49 ± 0.40*	3.22 ± 0.36	0.37 ± 0.18**	0.23 ± 0.22
70	2.95 ± 0.43*	3.57 ± 0.37	0.27 ± 0.18	0.16 ± 0.20
75	3.45 ± 0.47*	3.93 ± 0.44	0.16 ± 0.17	0.09 ± 0.16
80	3.88 ± 0.57*	4.24 ± 0.55	0.07 ± 0.14	0.04 ± 0.13

Table D5. Absolute CHO and fat oxidation rates for given exercise intensities at 50 vs. 100 rpm. *Significantly lower CHO than 100 rpm. **Significantly lower fat than 100 rpm.

$\dot{V}O_2 = a + b*intensity$				
	50 rpm		100 rpm	
No	a	b	a	b
1	281.67	39.03	1205.01	29.23
2	245.16	46.61	1171.48	38.89
3	476.16	35.54	758.30	31.79
4	354.17	30.97	1041.94	26.35
5	563.78	35.42	1214.04	35.17
6	429.05	32.54	1153.98	28.63
7	422.76	36.48	1873.21	23.58
8	386.46	36.81	930.19	31.15
9	625.08	30.91	822.15	28.85
10	456.05	28.50	719.57	27.57
11	380.52	50.57	799.29	47.04
Mean	420.08	36.67	1062.65	31.66
SD	111.35	6.71	328.01	6.59

Table D6. Fitting parameters of $\dot{V}O_2$ 50 vs. 100 rpm using a linear regression model.

			$\dot{V}CO_2 = ae^{b*intensity} + c$			
	50 rpm			**100 rpm**		
No	**a**	**b**	**c**	**a**	**b**	**c**
1	772.94	0.02	-86.97	2632.76	0.01	-1549.56
2	3346.03	0.01	-3143.56	5218.99	0.01	-4412.63
3	4015.59	0.01	-3602.32	4588.94	0.01	-4049.36
4	977.28	0.02	-518.56	3279.78	0.01	-2484.93
5	4109.55	0.01	-3767.79	11678.77	0.00	-10839.39
6	336.25	0.03	585.06	108.15	0.04	1703.26
7	2167.88	0.01	-1834.33	393.38	0.02	1586.02
8	1396.87	0.01	-871.79	2394.70	0.01	-1681.00
9	1665.04	0.01	-1144.65	2912.61	0.01	-2178.08
10	868.43	0.02	-336.34	82240.64	0.00	-81946.91
11	2534.67	0.01	-2134.85	1975.93	0.01	-1016.98
Mean	2017.32	0.01	-1532.37	10674.97	0.01	-9715.41
SD	1330.84	0.01	1481.54	23938.85	0.01	24192.92

Table D7. Fitting parameters of $\dot{V}CO_2$ at 50 vs. 100 rpm using a three parameters mono-exponential model.

			$BLC = ae^{b*intensity} + c$			
	50 rpm			**100 rpm**		
No	**a**	**b**	**c**	**a**	**b**	**c**
1	0.14	0.04	0.89	0.54	0.03	0.37
2	1.31	0.02	-1.60	0.07	0.05	1.21
3	0.17	0.04	1.01	0.05	0.06	1.40
4	0.03	0.06	1.25	0.50	0.03	0.42
5	0.10	0.04	0.58	0.78	0.03	-0.41
6	0.18	0.04	0.61	0.29	0.04	1.43
7	0.15	0.03	0.98	0.35	0.04	1.47
8	0.17	0.04	1.38	1.04	0.02	-0.12
9	0.11	0.04	0.53	0.41	0.03	0.93
10	0.37	0.03	0.17	0.36	0.04	1.02
11	0.01	0.07	0.64	0.03	0.06	0.98
Mean	0.25	0.04	0.58	0.40	0.04	0.79
SD	0.36	0.01	0.80	0.31	0.01	0.64

Table D8. Fitting parameters of BLC at 50 vs. 100 rpm using a three parameters mono-exponential model.

APPENDIX E

Subject No.	kel $(mmol.l^{-1})^2$ HG	r^2	kel $(mmol.l^{-1})^2$ NG	r^2
1	1.879	0.938	2.249	0.948
2	1.454	0.855	1.767	0.881
3	2.201	0.970	1.972	0.884
4	1.018	0.902	1.258	0.890
5	1.780	0.973	1.655	0.926
6	1.783	0.877	1.355	0.822
7	1.874	0.583	1.144	0.752
8	1.693	0.938	0.877	0.897
9	1.569	0.694	1.362	0.900
10	0.477	0.885	1.316	0.909
11	2.905	0.545	0.935	0.861
Mean ± SD	1.694 ± 0.618	0.833±0.15	1.445 ± 0.426	0.88±0.05

Table E1. Individual kel data for HG and NG protocols.

Intensity (%)	BLC for HG $(mmol.l^{-1})$	BLC for NG $(mmol.l^{-1})$
15	1.0 ± 0.3	0.93 ± 0.2
20	1.0 ± 0.3	1.01 ± 0.2
25	1.1 ± 0.3	1.09 ± 0.2
30	1.2 ± 0.3	1.20 ± 0.2
35	1.3 ± 0.3	1.33 ± 0.3
40	1.4 ± 0.4	1.48 ± 0.3

159

45	1.6 ± 0.4	1.66 ± 0.3
50	1.8 ± 0.5	1.88 ± 0.4
55	2.0 ± 0.6	2.15 ± 0.5
60	2.3 ± 7	2.47 ± 0.6
65	2.7 ± 0.8	2.85 ± 0.7
70	3.1 ± 1.0	3.32 ± 0.9
75	3.7 ± 1.1	3.88 ± 1.0
80	4.4 ± 1.3	4.56 ± 1.2
85	5.3 ± 1.5	5.38 ± 1.5
90	6.4 ± 1.8	6.39 ± 1.7
95	7.8 ± 2.0	7.60 ± 2.1

Table E2. BLC data at submaximal intensity levels for HG and NG protocols.

Intensity (%)	RPY (%)	RPY (%)	RFAT (%)	RFAT (%)
	HG	NG	HG	NG
15	36.74 ± 15.02	38.14 ± 9.76	63.26 ± 15.02	61.86 ± 9.76
20	39.37 ± 15.52	41.73 ± 9.51	60.63 ± 15.52	58.27± 9.51
25	42.37 ± 15.99	45.75 ± 9.47	7.63 ± 15.99	54.25 ± 9.47
30	45.75 ± 16.36	50.17 ± 9.63	54.25 ± 16.36	49.83 ± 9.63
35	49.53 ± 16.54	54.91 ± 9.91	50.47 ± 16.54	45.09 ± 9.91
40	53.70 ± 16.47	59.87 ± 10.21	46.30 ± 16.47	40.13 ± 10.21
45	58.22 ± 16.12	64.90 ± 10.46	41.78 ± 16.12	35.10 ± 10.46
50	63.02 ± 15.54	69.87 ± 10.56	36.98 ± 15.54	30.13 ± 10.56
55	67.96 ± 14.78	74.62 ± 10.43	32.04 ± 14.78	25.38 ± 10.43

60	72.89 ± 13.91	79.03 ± 10.02	27.11 ± 13.91	20.97± 10.02
65	77.63 ± 12.94	83.02 ± 9.31	22.37 ± 12.94	16.98 ± 9.31
70	82.03 ± 11.78	86.51 ± 8.32	17.97 ± 11.78	13.49 ± 8.32
75	86.00 ± 10.32	89.50 ± 7.15	14.00 ± 10.32	10.50 ± 7.15
80	89.46 ± 8.56	92.00 ± 5.90	10.54 ± 8.56	8.00 ± 5.90
85	92.38 ± 6.62	94.02 ± 4.69	7.62 ± 6.62	5.98 ± 4.69
90	94.73 ± 4.73	95.61 ± 3.58	5.27 ± 4.73	4.39 ± 3.58
95	96.50 ± 3.13	96.83 ± 2.65	3.50 ± 3.13	3.17 ± 2.65

Table E3. Relative rates of fat and CHO at given exercise intensities for HG and NG protocols.

Intensity (%)	CHO oxidation (g.min^{-1})		Fat oxidation (g.min^{-1})	
	HG	NG	HG	NG
15	0.40 ± 0.16	0.41 ± 0.12	0.29 ± 0.08	0.27 ± 0.05
20	0.51 ± 0.19	0.53 ± 0.13	0.33 ± 0.11	0.31 ± 0.07
25	0.63 ± 0.22	0.68 ± 0.14	0.37 ± 0.13	0.34 ± 0.08
30	0.77 ± 0.25	0.85 ± 0.15	0.39 ± 0.15	0.35 ± 0.10
35	0.94 ± 0.28	1.04 ± 0.18	0.41 ± 0.17	0.36 ± 0.11
40	1.13 ± 0.31	1.26 ± 0.21	0.41 ± 0.18	0.36 ± 0.13
45	1.34 ± 0.33	1.50 ± 0.25	0.41 ± 0.19	0.34 ± 0.14
50	1.58 ± 0.36	1.76 ± 0.30	0.39 ± 0.19	0.32 ± 0.14
55	1.85 ± 0.39	2.03 ± 0.35	0.37 ± 0.19	0.29 ± 0.15
60	2.13 ± 0.43	2.32 ± 0.41	0.34 ± 0.19	0.26 ± 0.14
65	2.43 ± 0.48	2.62 ± 0.47	0.30 ± 0.18	0.22 ± 0.14
70	2.75 ± 0.53	2.91 ± 0.52	0.25 ± 0.17	0.19 ± 0.13

75	3.06 ± 0.58	3.20 ± 0.58	0.21 ± 0.15	0.16 ± 0.11
80	3.37 ± 0.63	3.48 ± 0.64	0.16 ± 0.13	0.12 ± 0.09
85	3.67 ± 0.67	3.76 ± 0.69	0.12 ± 0.10	0.10 ± 0.08
90	3.95 ± 0.71	4.02 ± 0.74	0.09 ± 0.07	0.07 ± 0.06
95	4.23 ± 0.75	4.27 ± 0.80	0.06 ± 0.05	0.06 ± 0.05

Table E4. Absolute fat and CHO oxidation rates at given exercise intensities for HG and NG protocols.

Lightning Source UK Ltd.
Milton Keynes UK
UKOW03f1548211013

219469UK00001B/34/P